ZEITGESCHICHTE

Ehrenpräsidentin:
em. Univ.-Prof. Dr. Erika Weinzierl († 2014)

Herausgeber:
Univ.-Prof. DDr. Oliver Rathkolb

Redaktion:
em. Univ.-Prof. Dr. Rudolf Ardelt (Linz), ao. Univ.-Prof.[in] Mag.[a] Dr.[in] Ingrid Bauer (Salzburg/ Wien), SSc Mag.[a] Dr.[in] Ingrid Böhler (Innsbruck), Dr.[in] Lucile Dreidemy (Toulouse), Prof. Dr. Michael Gehler (Hildesheim), ao. Univ.-Prof. i. R. Dr. Robert Hoffmann (Salzburg), ao. Univ.-Prof. Dr. Michael John / Koordination (Linz), Assoz. Prof.[in] Dr.[in] Birgit Kirchmayr (Linz), Dr. Oliver Kühschelm (Wien), Univ.-Prof. Dr. Ernst Langthaler (Linz), Dr.[in] Ina Markova (Wien), Univ.-Prof. Mag. Dr. Wolfgang Mueller (Wien), Univ.-Prof. Dr. Bertrand Perz (Wien), Univ.-Prof. Dr. Dieter Pohl (Klagenfurt), Dr.[in] Lisa Rettl (Wien), Univ.-Prof. Mag. Dr. Dirk Rupnow (Innsbruck), Mag.[a] Adina Seeger (Wien), Ass.-Prof. Mag. Dr. Valentin Sima (Klagenfurt), Prof.[in] Dr.[in] Sybille Steinbacher (Frankfurt am Main), Dr. Christian H. Stifter / Rezensionsteil (Wien), Univ.-Doz.[in] Mag.[a] Dr.[in] Heidemarie Uhl (Wien/Graz), Gastprof. (FH) Priv.-Doz. Mag. Dr. Wolfgang Weber, MA, MAS (Vorarlberg), Mag. Dr. Florian Wenninger (Wien), Assoz.-Prof.[in] Mag.[a] Dr.[in] Heidrun Zettelbauer (Graz).

Peer-Review Committee (2018–2020):
Ass.-Prof.[in] Mag.[a] Dr.[in] Tina Bahovec (Institut für Geschichte, Universität Klagenfurt), Prof. Dr. Arnd Bauerkämper (Fachbereich Geschichts- und Kulturwissenschaften, Freie Universität Berlin), Günter Bischof, Ph.D. (Center Austria, University of New Orleans), Dr.[in] Regina Fritz (Institut für Zeitgeschichte, Universität Wien/Historisches Institut, Universität Bern), ao. Univ.-Prof.[in] Mag.[a] Dr.[in] Johanna Gehmacher (Institut für Zeitgeschichte, Universität Wien), Univ.-Prof. i. R. Dr. Hanns Haas (Universität Salzburg), Univ.-Prof. i. R. Dr. Ernst Hanisch (Salzburg), Univ.-Prof.[in] Mag.[a] Dr.[in] Gabriella Hauch (Institut für Geschichte, Universität Wien), Univ.-Doz. Dr. Hans Heiss (Institut für Zeitgeschichte, Universität Innsbruck), Robert G. Knight, Ph.D. (Department of Politics, History and International Relations, Loughborough University), Dr.[in] Jill Lewis (University of Wales, Swansea), Prof. Dr. Oto Luthar (Slowenische Akademie der Wissenschaften, Ljubljana), Hon.-Prof. Dr. Wolfgang Neugebauer (Dokumentationsarchiv des Österreichischen Widerstandes, Wien), Mag. Dr. Peter Pirker (Institut für Staatswissenschaft, Universität Wien), Prof. Dr. Markus Reisenleitner (Department of Humanities, York University, Toronto), Dr.[in] Elisabeth Röhrlich (Institut für Geschichte, Universität Wien), ao. Univ.-Prof.[in] Dr.[in] Karin M. Schmidlechner-Lienhart (Institut für Geschichte/Zeitgeschichte, Universität Graz), Univ.-Prof. i. R. Mag. Dr. Friedrich Stadler (Wien), Assoc.-Prof. Dr. Gerald Steinacher (University of Nebraska), Assoz.-Prof. DDr. Werner Suppanz (Institut für Geschichte/Zeitgeschichte, Universität Graz), Univ.-Prof. Dr. Philipp Ther, MA (Institut für Osteuropäische Geschichte, Universität Wien), Prof. Dr. Stefan Troebst (Leibniz-Institut für Geschichte und Kultur des östlichen Europa, Universität Leipzig), Prof. Dr. Michael Wildt (Institut für Geschichtswissenschaften, Humboldt-Universität zu Berlin).

zeitgeschichte
46. Jg., Heft 2 (2019)

The Memory of Guilt Revisited. The Slovenian Post-Socialist Remembrance Landscape in Transition

Edited by
Oto Luthar and Heidemarie Uhl

V&R unipress

Vienna University Press

Contents

Heidemarie Uhl
Editorial 177

Oto Luthar
Introduction 179

Artikel

Marta Verginella
Political Remake of Slovenian History and Trivialisation of Memory . . . 189

Bojan Godeša
Slovenian Historiography in the Grip of Reconciliation 205

Marko Zajc
The Politics of Memory in Slovenia and the Erection of the Monument to
the Victims of All Wars 225

Maruša Pušnik
Media-Based Historical Revisionism and the Public's Memories of the
Second World War 241

Oto Luthar
The Sanitation of Slovenian Post-Socialist Memorial Landscape 261

zeitgeschichte extra

Petra Mayrhofer
Searching for "1989" on the Transnational Remembrance Landscape:
A Topography 277

Abstracts 295

Rezensionen

Brigitte Entner
Robert Knight, Slavs in Post-Nazi Austria 301

Heimo Gruber
Alfred Pfoser/Andreas Weigl, Die erste Stunde Null 303

Franz Mathis
Günter Bischof/Hans Petschar, Der Marshallplan 306

Autor/inn/en 309

Heidemarie Uhl

Editorial

The collapse of the communist states is regarded as the starting point of the new Europe. With this turning point, historical narratives have had to be rewritten in the post-socialist countries. While the destruction of Communist monuments is imprinted on European collective memory as a visual icon reflecting this caesura, the much more complex process of opening up and diversifying the writing of history has drawn little attention. This also holds true for the nationalist and revisionist backlash in dealing with traumatic historical events, which tends to be highlighted only in the context of specific, particularly dramatic political interventions and measures, such as the marginalization of the Holocaust by the House of Terror in Budapest or the Polish Memory Laws.

Focusing on the little known case of Slovenia, this issue of *zeitgeschichte* offers a comprehensive survey of the transformations affecting collective memory and the writing of history in one post-communist country. We are very pleased to have won Oto Luthar, arguably the most distinguished Slovenian exponent of a form of memory history that meets international scholarly standards, as guest editor. His introduction and the essays in this issue analyze the ways in which Slovenian society has grappled with traumatic historical events. The authors pointedly probe the fields of history politics, memorial culture and the writing of history against the background of the Europe-wide changes in the construction of memory. Specific microhistories allow for an analysis of relevant controversies and political interventions in the struggle over the interpretation of Slovenia's past. Given the proliferating illiberal tendencies in the political culture of numerous European countries, which threaten to curtail critical scholarly discussions of the dominant versions of national history, the strategies of historical revisionism described in this issue are likely to be of considerable interest not only to scholars interested specifically in the case of Slovenia.

Oto Luthar

Introduction

After 1989, the impact of historical representation on forming new democracies has become an inseparable part of the new politics of history in post-socialist societies. According to Charles S. Maier, discussion about the changing "architecture of historical knowledge"[1] also took place in certain other European countries. Even more so, the new "hunger for memory"[2] became "a remarkable cultural feature" across Western Europe. Indeed memory, and particularly memory relating to *the century of extremes*, has become a subject of contemplation in its own right rather than the mere subject of the past. This change was not confined to the late 1980s, and it took place well beyond the bounds of Western Europe. To some extent, it was even the societies of the "Eastern Bloc" that experienced "an era of self-archaeologization."[3] The latter was particularly true for Yugoslavia and – within it – Slovenia. Therefore, the editors of this volume, much like Marta Verginella in her contribution, aim to draw attention to the aftermath of the so-called nationalization of the past, or the fact that the professional debate over the nature of historical explanation, which started in the 1980s, has largely been overshadowed by new attempts to monopolize historical interpretation. The once vivid interest in new forms of historical representation has given way to the politicized reinterpretation of national histories in all countries of the former Yugoslavia. In Slovenian historiography, the euphoria that accompanied the struggle for independence opened the way for a steamroller of positivist nationalism that flattened almost every hint of interpretational polyphony. The debate that started in the early 1980s following the first critical articles on socialist historiography,[4] and the first translations of relevant theo-

---

1 Alun Munslow, *The New History* (Harlow: Pearson Longman, 2003), 1.
2 Charles S. Maier, *The Unmasterable Past. History, Holocaust, and German National Identity* (Cambridge: Harvard University Press, 1988), 149.
3 Ibid., 123.
4 Vodopivec, Peter. "Poskus opredelitve razvoja slovenskega zgodovonopisja z vidika zgodovina-ideologija" [A Tentative Definition of the Development of Slovenian Historiography in Light of the Relationship between History and Ideology], *Problemi*, November 1, 1984.

retical considerations regarding the nature of historical interpretation,⁵ has largely been replaced by the nationalist interpretation of national cultural heritage. Consequently, the anticipated democratization and (post)modernization of historical interpretation have been obstructed by yet another monopolization of historical interpretation, followed by a new political monopolization of a certain kind of historical interpretation. The change was, and still is, closely connected with Slovenian revisionist and negationist currents. It is based on a more or less archaic understanding of the postmodern view of history as an authoring process, while most historians have actually never stopped believing history to be a straightforward interpretative report of factual findings. In their mystification of the national past, history thus remains an interpretational and politically inspired project rather than the result of uncertainties of meanings created "through the exercise of our own mind."⁶ Even more so, the revisionists deliberately use a narrow understanding of history to place their politicized interpretation on the agenda as completely relevant and legitimate.

Therefore, the academic colleagues⁷ who were invited to participate in this special volume were particularly encouraged to engage in fields where the dynamics of change in dealing with the politics of memory in Slovenia can be observed. In their own distinctive ways and with various disciplinary focal points, the contributors were asked to rethink 1) the emergence of the new politics of memory; that is, post-communist historiographies, particularly in relation to the question of possible political involvement in interpreting the past and its effects on discussing the theory and philosophy of history; 2) the nationalization of the past by reinventing "authentic national historical memory"; and 3) the mediatization of traumatic history (or a traumatic past) by using new communication technologies.

From these focal points, the authors – from the University of Ljubljana, the Institute of Contemporary History, and the Research Center of the Slovenian Academy of Sciences and Arts – address the relationship between various modes of post-communist enactments of memory and representations of the past.

Like other former communist countries, Slovenia has also been witnessing –

---

5 See for example Oto Luthar, *Vsi Tukididovi možje. Sodobne teorije zgodovinopisja* (Ljubljana: Krt, 1990).
6 Alun Munslow, *The New History* (Harlow: Pearson Longman, 2003), 34.
7 The invited authors have participated in the debate on the post-socialist politics of memory for at least ten years, and three of them have dealt with the topic for almost two decades. When thinking of also inviting authors pushing for the radical reinterpretation of the historical period under discussion, it became clear that over the last twenty-five years, their interpretation more or less merged with their ideological perspective. Instead of openly discussing questions of objectivity, truth and causation, they still believe that historical truth resides in justified descriptive statements that correspond to the empirical reconstruction of human intentionality, while some of them turned into political commentators.

since the second half of the 1990s – a politically motivated radical reinterpretation of the most traumatic periods of national history. The brief period of attempts toward symbolic reconciliation, a period that was underscored by a special meeting between Slovenia's first president, Milan Kučan, and the Archbishop of Ljubljana Alojzij Šuštar,[8] boiled down to a fierce struggle over the past. A country whose population had fought tooth and nail to distance itself from the Balkans two decades or so later witnessed the entrenchment of what, according to the Slovenian diplomat Vojko Volk, is particularly characteristic of this part of Europe. In his opinion, Slovenia, too, has become known as a part of the world "where historians deal with politics and politicians with history."[9]

While in contrast to Croatia, Serbia, and Bosnia & Herzegovina, only few Slovenian historians ended up in politics, but they crucially contributed to a polarization in the understanding of the period during and after the Second World War; a polarization that was triggered by a systematic reversal of the roles of victims and perpetrators, and a fitful advocacy of "functional" collaboration with the German and Italian forces. As in other processes of this kind, the Slovenian material and interpretative *sanitization*[10] of the Second World War and its aftermath started almost immediately after independence. The material-symbolic sanitization includes the desecration of the Jewish section of Ljubljana's central cemetery, the destruction of memorial pillars tracing the barbed wire fence that enclosed occupied Ljubljana in 1942–1943, and the erection of monuments to the "victims of communist violence." The symbolic sanitization, on the other hand, comprises historiographical reinterpretations of interwar developments, with an emphasis on the rehabilitation of local collaboration with the Fascist and Nazi occupation forces.

Since 2014, the new landscape of memory started to systematically translate the members of the Partisan resistance movement, hostages, and civilian casu-

---

8 At the ceremony, organized by the Slovenian Presidency, Milan Kučan explicitly acknowledged the accountability of the communist government for the postwar killings by concluding with the best speech he delivered in all of his entire presidential terms, stating: "Here they were killing us. Here we were killing each other. Here we were fighting and hiding against violence. Here we were winning and hiding the evil that was caused by our fighting and winning. Here victory often turned into defeat. Let us say to each other: here, where the bones are scattered of all who were fighting for this or that truth, with this or that thought, is the right place for reconciliation, which we need as a nation looking forward into the future. For what happened, we are sincerely regretful. Let us end it, here and now. It was." (http://www.bivsi-predsednik.si/up-rs/2002-2007/bp-mk.nsf/dokumenti/08.07.1990-90-92)
9 Vojko Volk, "Zgodovina, nočna mora Balkana," *Sobotna priloga Dela* (August 15, 2018): 15. The complete sentence is as follows: "In fact, the Balkans is wherever historians deal with politics and politicians deal with history."
10 I have decided to use the term sanitization because of the way in which Slovenian revisionists were meticulously separating and deleting facts that would endanger their reinterpretation of the 1930s, the Second World War, and the period immediately after the war.

alties into perpetrators, while portraying collaborationist troops as victims. From that point on, all those who have opposed this reinvention have been dismissed as "arch-revisionists," "arch-manipulators," and "fired-up philo-communist diehards." Instead of the previous balancing of guilt and the reframing of occupation and resistance against it into civil war, the revised or sanitized interpretation simply reversed the roles of victims and perpetrators. Even more so, according to the authors of the revised national history, in 1945 Slovenia did not enter a period of freedom, but one of "dictatorship", whose proponents continue to dominate the media space even after independence. One of the authors who has been consistently supportive of the radical interpretation of this part of history goes even as far as to talk of "an underground coup", or a coup by "the former UDBA"; that is, the former secret police.[11] This provided the reason for one of the papers in this volume to investigate the mediatization of the past, as most discussions take place in daily newspapers and on various television channels, including national television. In recent years, this has been the medium where revisionists[12] have discussed "communist dictatorship" and "the Slovenian Holocaust."[13]

However, rather than offering specific case studies, the authors of this volume are more interested in the use of language and the modes of historicization in which revisionists follow the "creative response concept,"[14] claiming that one should never let the facts get in the way of intended interpretation.

---

11 Jože Možina,"Žal mi je, vse je res," *Sobotna priloga Dela* (August 18, 2018): 20. Although the UDBA (Serbo-Croatian: *Uprava državne bezbednosti*) had a Slovenian branch of the State Security Administration (the UDV, or *Uprava državne varnosti*), authors like Možina prefer to use the Serbo-Croatian name, stressing the interpretation that communism was an import from Soviet Russia, and from other parts of Yugoslavia.
12 Here the term *(historical) revisionism* is understood as a practice of radical reinterpretation of the past that is unequally founded on the penchant for therapeutic values over cognitive values. Like Aviezer Tucker, I understand this as revised historiography immune to the effect of evidence; see Aviezer Tucker, "Historiographic Revision and Revisionism: The Evidential Difference," in *Past in the Making: Historical Revisionism in Central Europe After 1989*, edited by Michal Kopeček (Budapest: CEU Press, 2008), 3. Furthermore, the term is used here to describe the process of the post-communist radical reinterpretation of the most traumatic aspects of the past of Eastern European countries in the twentieth century. The term is, needless to say, inadequate. However, for the time being, I see no alternatives. The terms *negationism, the monopolization of memory, the distortion of history, rewriting, reinventing, redefining, re-evaluating, re-reading, abusing, erasing, changing, colonizing*, and … *the past* do not cover the full spectrum; therefore, the search for a more adequate term continues.
13 The term "Slovenian Holocaust" is frequently used by Slovenian right-wing politicians. One such politician is also the former president of parliament, Dr. France Cukjati, from 2016 the president of the revisionist right-wing platform Zbor za republiko/Core for the Republic. See also Matjaž Gruden, "'Slovenski holokavst' ali kako manipulira zborovodja mopedšova za republiko," in *Hokuspokus*, August 29, 2019.
14 The best proof of this concept's scope and impact is the public relations company with the same sounding name, which has a focus on issue advocacy. According to their website

This issue has received detailed consideration in Maruša Pušnik's article, especially in terms of how the memories of the Second World War are mediatized. Pušnik analyses historical revisionism in the media within the context of wider sociopolitical history-making processes in Slovenia. As her analysis determines, the mainstream media fuel memory battles in Slovenian public space, create revisionist narratives of the Second World War, and thus prompt audiences to erase old memories and create new ones. The forced forgetting of the Second World War, promoted by the current media discursive regime, also coincides with popular memories and the politics of bottom-up memory. In her opinion, such a politics of memory obscures the paradigm of the liberators and the aggressors, and influences the popular perception of developments that took place during and after the war.

Proceeding from Hannah Arendt's reflection on the political use of history (in *Truth and Politics*), Marta Verginella deals with the controversial relationship between historical truth and its political distortions. In her view, the strong political and public uses of history in Slovenia coexist with fundamental processes and transitions within Slovenian society. The Slovenian "memory boom" is in some aspects similar to what took place in the Yugoslav area, and in other European countries. On the other hand, Verginella points out certain specific aspects of the Slovenian politics of the past, claiming that the post-communist interest in "all victims" does not include the latest historical research, but tends to be substituted by a political-memorializing plan in which the victims are increasingly enveloped in a kind of sacredness and power.

The concept of national reconciliation is part of this enveloping, and this is the topic of Bojan Godeša's article. Beginning with the introduction of the concept to Slovenia in the 1980s, the author believes the idea of national reconciliation to be a suitable basis for transcending internal disparities. On the other hand, he shares the belief that the ideology of reconciliation affirms a specific type of historical revisionism, whose central point is a total silence regarding pre-war confessional and ideological anti-Semitism by the Slovenian Catholic Church and its close ally, the Slovenian People's Party. Similarly to Irena Šumi, he believes that the ideology of reconciliation likewise totally suppresses the wartime persecution of Slovenian Jews at the hands of the collaborationist authorities, as well as the post-war programmatic anti-Semitism of the revolutionary authorities. With this complete omission, the idea of reconciliation not only entirely

---

presentation, this is all "about shaping public opinion and creating success." Their latest project is related to the nomination of Brett Kavanaugh for the US Supreme Court.

missed its declared goal of "accepting our history", but decontextualized the history itself – and in so doing, distorted it.¹⁵

When talking about the ways in which a society remembers past traumatic events and processes such as the Second World War and post-war killings, for Marko Zajc the question is not only what is being discussed, but also what discourse or set of concepts is being used.¹⁶ According to his analysis of recent literature in Slovenia, one of the most frequently used concepts is that of "transitional justice",¹⁷ which is found in legal and political science literature on the topic, as well as in publications by non-governmental organizations.¹⁸

The main focus of Zajc's article, however, is on the newest monument dedicated to the "victims of all wars", which was unveiled in the summer of 2017. Because the event was eagerly commented on by all political parties, public intellectuals, and the media, he is particularly interested in the media reflections that focused on what currently seems to be the prevailing signifier. Alongside this, Zajc is convinced that emptiness is truly the main characteristic of the monument. The viewpoint of the monument clearly manifests the ideology of Slovenian national dissension, or its division into two more or less equal parts.

By analysing changes in the post-communist memorial landscape of Slovenia after 1991, Oto Luthar focuses on the latest shift in this process. According to his analysis, the first twenty years after the end of communism were marked by an ambition to redistribute responsibility (and blame) for the civil war by placing responsibility squarely on the Slovenian Partisans. After 2014, however, the memorials demand a more radical reinterpretation. According to their inscriptions, the Partisans and the civilian victims of the Nazis and Fascists are to be understood as perpetrators, whereas the members of collaborationist units, organized as the Home Guard, are praised as members of a Slovenian National Army.

The second part of Luthar's analysis looks at US involvement in this process. In 2014, the former US ambassador to Slovenia initiated the installing of the commemorative plaque that describes Nazi and Fascist collaborators as "Slovenians [...] who sought peace but could not avoid war."¹⁹ In so doing, the

---

15 See also Irena Šumi, "Slovenski antisemitizem, živ pokopan v ideologiji slovenske narodne sprave," ČKZ – Časopis za kritiko znanosti, 43, (2015) 260: 69–84.
16 Reinhart Koselleck, Vergangene Zukunft. Zur Semantik geschichtlicher Zeiten (Frankfurt am Main: Suhrkamp, 1995), 107–130.
17 Jon Elster, Closing the Books. Transitional Justice in Historical Perspective (Cambridge: Cambridge University Press, 2004), 77.
18 Olivera Simić and Zala Volčič (eds.), Transitional Justice and Civil Society in the Balkans (New York: Springer, 2013), 1.
19 The address in its entirety went further: besides transforming the perpetrators into victims, the deputy ambassador invited the audience gathered in front of the embassy in August 2016

mission not only reinterpreted the most traumatic part of modern Slovenian history, but also became directly involved in the Slovenian politics of the past.

All the authors in this volume, however, share Foucault's belief that discourses are not simply presentations, but also constitute practices of power because they play an active part in the formation of the phenomena of which they speak. In addition, we are even more aware that a significant portion of Slovenian historiography, be it positivist or objectivist, has always been predominantly marked by the seal of national ideology. For these authors, not to mention the negationists, historical writing inherited from the nineteenth century still offers a very credible model of pure scholarly thought.

"to honor and celebrate" the Slovenian negationists as "those who honestly seek reconciliation" and "strive to preserve Slovenia's independence and identity."

Artikel

Marta Verginella

Political Remake of Slovenian History and Trivialisation of Memory

Premise

In *Truth and Politics* (1967), Hannah Arendt examined the political uses to which history was put, inviting us to reflect on the contentious relationship between truth and politics and, above all, on the distortions or negations of certain truths deployed and defended by politics. If recourse to falsehood seems compatible with politics, not only in totalitarian regimes but also in western democracies (some of Arendt's observations referred to the use of falsehood in the United States' politics of image during the Vietnam War), it is because it has always been considered a necessary and legitimate political tool. As she pointed out: 'No one has ever doubted that truth and politics are on rather bad terms with each other, and no one, as far as I know, has ever counted truthfulness among the political virtues. Lies have always been regarded as necessary and justifiable tools not only of the politician's or the demagogue's but also of the statesman's trade.'[1]

The scholar's concern is not so much with the habit politicians have of preferring opinions to facts; rather, it is with the negation and perversion of every kind of truth and with the lack of respect on the part of politics for the 'truth of the fact', no less than the capacity of politics to distort and manipulate that truth even in cases where society has documentary proof to the contrary. That said, it is often society itself that prefers this kind of approach, and is prepared to support those politicians capable of adapting the facts to meet the expectations of their supporters. Faced with the self-deception practised by the political class for the 'common good', as has happened in the American case, it should be culture that takes up defence of the truth and interrupts this vicious circle that exists between politics and society.

Way back in 1967, Arendt's confidence in the 'guardians' of the truth, in scholars, intellectuals and judges, and in the capacity of academic culture to

---

1 Hannah Arendt, *Truth and Politics* (New York, London, Victoria, Toronto, Auckland: Penguin Books, 2000), 545.

correct political action can appear somewhat ingenuous today. Not only because the means at the disposal of academic culture have been, and continue to be, considerably reduced in favour of the mass media and social networks in recent decades, but also because part of the world of culture itself, whose aim should be to discover, protect and interpret the truth of the fact, tends to bend to the demands of the political and public abuse of history. Simplified readings of the recent past and historical narratives that propose easy analogies with structurally different historical phenomena (and that are nevertheless interested in uncovering 'new-old' political subjects) are taking hold, not only in marginal areas of forums and blogs, but even in historiographical and academic environments. The obsession with *making everything visible* and with bringing to light the traumas of the 20th century do not necessarily produce a greater or more complex awareness of the past, of ourselves, or of others.[2]

Since the end of the 1980s, and with greater insistence since the 1990s, there have been discussions in various European contexts concerning the political and public use and abuse of history, the importance of memory as it relates to oblivion,[3] the negative effects of an excessive amplification of remembrance at the expense of forgetting, and how new remembrance practices are often an answer to powerful demands for ideological repositioning from promoters of new political and national genealogies. That the promotion of these practices have something to do with research into new political points of reference is evident above all in those European contexts in which there is a greater need to 'forget' pre-transition political associations and those affiliations that have now become obsolete.

After the fall of the Berlin Wall, the interpretations and representations of the past that had been developed during the World War II and remained in force until the 1980s proved to be no longer appropriate. In the former communist world in particular, the 'remake of the world', as Istvan Rév defined it analysing the Hungarian case, became unavoidable: 'certainties, the pillars of life had gone; familiar recurring events, the rhythm of existence, ordinary days and holidays, the well-known street names, the social significance of the neighbourhood, the significance of photographs in the family album, social capital, the knowledge of Russian as a foreign language to be used, the value of the sociometric network of

---

2 Manuel Cruz, *I brutti scherzi del passato, Identità, responsabilità, storia* (Torino: Bollati Boringhieri, 2010), 16–17.
3 Both remembering and forgetting are objects of cultural contraction. The dialectical relationship between the two takes place within a determined collectivity, and is conditioned by power balances and by those who write history (Idith Zertal, *Israele e la Shoah. La nazione e il culto della tragedia* (Torino: Einaudi, 2000), 43.

one's own private and professional world, the stability of memories, the comprehension of private and public history.'[4]

In common with other countries of Eastern Europe, Hungary abandoned those accounts that had sought to create a common and shared identity under the banner of communist ideology, along with 'the horizon within which national history in the decades following World War II was perceived',[5] in an effort to restore the national continuity that had been interrupted by World War II and by communism. In the case of Yugoslavia, the narrative of the 'War of Liberation', which had been the source of legitimisation and identity for the Socialist Federal Republic of Yugoslavia, as well as one of the cornerstones of socialist regimes until the 1980s, began to be gradually abandoned as the ideological glue that had bound together the nations of Yugoslavia cracked and the victims of revolutionary and communist violence gradually resurfaced at the centre of the public debate. The act of remembrance of wartime and post-war massacres began to be transformed ever more clearly into a condemnation of Tito's regime, and to be included in the collective memory of all those experiences that the Yugoslav population had undergone during and after World War II and that had remained concealed for more than 40 years.[6] In the public debate and in the Yugoslav history books published before the 1990s, space had been made for the partisans and for the heroes of the War of Liberation; the defeated remained outside the official narrative, relegated to individual and family memories. The experiences of deportations to Nazi camps and internments in Fascist camps remained at the margins of collective memory; and although they were occasionally remembered and testimonies were collected, they did not enter the official context developed to commemorate the partisan epic. The multiplication of memories and an ever-more intense process of historical revisiting in the Yugoslav context not only opened new spaces for democracy, but also served to justify new acts of violence.[7] Some of the subjects excluded from the historical narrative in force in Yugoslavia until the end of the 1980s became promoters of new forms of collective memory, and their moral ransom demands encountered new interested political listeners to represent them.

If we compare the new forms of public memory installed since the 1990s in the

---

4 István Rév, *Giustizia retroattiva, Preistoria del comunismo* (Milano: Feltrinelli, 2007), 19.
5 Alfredo Laudiero, *Oltre il nazionalismo. Le nuove storiografie dell'est* (Naples: L'ancora del Mediterraneo, 2004), 24.
6 During the communist period, around 100,000 people were executed without trial in the territory of present-day Slovenia in 1945 and 1946, and buried in more than 600 secret mass graves. Approximately 14,000 of them were Slovenes, the rest were Croats, Serbs, Montenegrins and Germans.
7 Wolfgang Höpken, "Tra politica della memoria e lutto: ricordare la Seconda guerra mondiale in Jugoslavia," *Cattive memorie. Luoghi, simboli e narrazioni delle guerre nei Balcani. Diario europeo*, I/2008: 30.

former Yugoslavia with those that have appeared in other European countries, we see that the equilibrium established between oblivion and memory has always been linked to demands made by single political subjects, i. e. defenders of the interests of those defeated during World War II and also, in Eastern Europe, of those who had been distanced from positions of power after the establishment of communism. In this context, mention should be made of the link created between the victims of 20th century bloodshed and their supporters through the various attempts made to obtain material and moral redress – a link which, regardless of the specificity of the single context that generated it, denotes a community of interaction between memory, history and politics.[8] This signals a clear change of direction by those memory-related practices that occur in a society in which the number of people prepared to apportion blame increases, while the number of people prepared to take responsibility or blame upon themselves grows smaller.[9]

In a society affected by 'commemorative bulimia' and increasingly tempted by innocence, openness to self-incrimination and the assumption of ethical responsibility effectively decreases at the same time as conditions favourable to victim discourse are created. Valentina Pisanty, efficiently highlighting this tendency to give greater centrality to victims, explains that 'the symbolic condition of Victim is paraded as an honorary title, a generator of social prestige and moral capital'. The victim is not seen as a traumatised person who is to be helped to reintegrate into everyday life, but rather as a representative 'of a universal and permanent psychological condition'.[10] The revival of the victim mechanism is the privilege of not only of the survivors, as David Bidussa clearly points out, 'but also and increasingly of those who have a paranoid vision of reality, obsessed by the idea of powerful forces that act against their own people. An affirmation of the process of producing victims that eliminates the historical and factual dimension of its realisation in terms of acts, conflicts, figures, circumstances.'[11]

In the Slovenian case with which we are concerned, a strong political and public use of history exists alongside practices that foster oblivion concerning the historically fundamental processes and transitions of Slovenian society. The Slovenian 'memory boom' is in some respects similar to that which took place in Yugoslavia and in other European countries (particularly in ex-communist countries after the political changes of the late 1980s and early 1990s). However,

---

8 On the elective relationship between the historian and power, cf. Aldo Giannuli, *L'abuso pubblico della storia* (Parma: Guanda, 2009), 18.
9 Manuel Cruz, *I brutti scherzi del passato. Identità, responsabilità, storia* (Torino: Bollati Boringhieri, 2010), 70.
10 Valentina Pisanty, *Abusi di memoria. Negare, banalizzare, sacralizzare la Shoah* (Milano: Bruno Mondadori, 2012), 6.
11 David Bidussa, *Dopo l'ultimo testimone* (Torino: Einaudi, 2009).

it has also had certain specific aspects that I will seek to point out. The demand, backed by political will, for space to be given to the memory of the victims has not been translated in Slovenia into a need to grant equal respect to all innocent victims of political violence and to their memory. Moreover, the attention paid to victims has not automatically been transformed into a demand for greater historiographical examination, since in the commemorative context the plan for historical knowledge tends to be substituted by a political-memorial plan in which the victims are increasingly invested with a kind of sacredness and power.[12]

The ambivalent and conflicting features of history have been sanitised to make them suit the new narrative offered at official and public occasions.[13] The lack of an extension of historiographical investigation, at least until the end of the 1990s, suited very precise political choices, and therefore permitted those subjects to be hidden that, if investigated, would have made it possible to understand that 'mass violence [was] the result of a complex interweaving of three protagonists: executioners, victims and bystanders, meaning the "grey area" found in the middle and whose behaviour often decides the outcome of a conflict.'[14] When one proceeds from this statement, as Enzo Traverso observes, then one is forced to 'recognize that giving exclusive attention to the memory of the victims risks distorting the reading of an event.'[15]

Forgetful society, divided memories

In Slovenian society, which in terms of its demographical and geographical dimensions can be defined as a *face-to-face* society, it is not difficult to reconstruct the circuits forged between politics and history, between commemorative practices and political subjects, as well as the ways and times with which the mass media (and historiography itself) have favoured the rewriting of the recent past. In this paper, I will seek to identify some of the salient lines of practices of this type and to explain the reasons why they are activated. I will also take a brief look at the role that memory, both individual and collective, has played (and still plays) in the practice of rewriting Slovenian history, above all that of World War II and the post-war period.

For at least some decades, the recent Yugoslav past has been the object of geopolitical analysis and of sociological and historiographic commentary that

---

12 Cf. Zertal, *Israele la Shoah*, cit. VIII.
13 Marcela Ravenna, *Carnefici e vittime* (Bologna: Il Mulino, 2004), 92.
14 Enzo Traverso, *A ferro e a fuoco. La guerra civile europea 1914–1945* (Bologna: Il Mulino, 2007), 11.
15 Traverso, *A ferro e a fuoco*, 11.

converges in identifying, in the exploitable and political use of history, one of the assumptions of nationalistic euphoria that preceded and accompanied the bloodbath in the Balkan Peninsula.[16] At the beginning of the 1990s, of all the republics of the former Yugoslavia, Slovenia found itself to be the one least subject to the politically instrumental use of history, with the political and institutional changes peacefully brought about from the end of the 1980s helping to immunise it somewhat from the horrors taking place elsewhere in the region. Slovenia also seemed to be the least prone to easy revisionism and to revisiting its recent past in an exclusively nationalistic key. After ten years of independence, however, history was proving to be an essential tool for nourishing a strong national identity, as well as becoming the main tool for delegitimising the centre-left political forces then in government, which have been claimed to represent continuity with the Yugoslav past.[17] Now, almost three decades on from the creation of the Slovenian state, contemporary Slovenian history continues to be not only one of the privileged spaces of political confrontation, but also the device and principal motive by which, in many cases, the delegitimisation of political subjects is activated and realised.

Concerning this, we should note the regret often expressed by important representatives of the centre-right and of the Slovenian Church concerning the fact that the country has not, since independence, carried out a process of political purging (*lustration*) and has therefore not removed from important public and institutional offices all those supporters and representatives of the past regime.[18] There have been numerous cases of a casual and manipulative use of documentation emanating from the files of the Yugoslav secret service (UDBA), which have been conveniently cleansed above all of those documents that could have compromised members of the old establishment who had remained active during the transition period. Those who benefited most from this were those political players who, when changing their affiliation, repudiated their own communist past, passing themselves off as representing the new present. In more than one case, documentation preserved in the UDBA archives was revealed in court to have been improperly used to politically discredit in-

---

16 On the instrumentalisation of history in the Yugoslav context, see Hrvoje Glavač, *Prošlost je teško pitanje* (Zagreb: Friedrich-Naumann-Stiftung, 2000); Igor Graovac, Igor (ed.), *Dijalog povjesničara/istoričara* (Zagreb: Friedrich-Naumann-Stiftung, 2005); Nebojša Popov (ed.), "*Srpska strana rata*; Trauma i katarza u istorijskom pamćenju," *Migracijske i etničke teme*, 20 (4), December 2004.

17 Marta Verginella, "Il peso della storia in Fra invenzione della tradizione e ri-scrittura del passato. La storiografia slovena degli anni Novanta," *Qualestoria*, XXVII (1999) 1: 9–34.

18 The advocates of *lustration* do not, however, specify exactly which categories of person should have been considered, leaving its eventual implementation suspended. This was also certainly because implementation would have had serious consequences for the top echelons of the centre-right, which comprises persons whose communist militancy was marked.

dividual public personalities[19] whose main defect was to be in open disagreement with the political forces of the centre-right and, in particular, with the SDS party[20] of Janez Janša, in his youth a notable member of the League of Communists and today a fervent anti-communist.

As an example of this tendency, the day of remembrance organised on 7 October 2012 to commemorate the post-war massacres at Teharje[21] is worth mentioning. On that occasion, while the ex-bishop of Koper Metod Pirih underlined the necessity of giving a name and a surname to every victim and of restoring to memory all those who had not had the right to be buried, Boštjan Zadnikar, representative of *Nova slovenska zaveza* (New Slovenian Commitment), an organisation known for its 'militant anti-communism',[22] used far more inflammatory terms, declaring that Slovenia, still infested with neo-Bolshevism, needed external spiritual and moral arbitration, and that the future of the nation was uncertain precisely because the population were forced to live alongside neo-Bolsheviks; according to Zadnikar, this 'accursed revolution' meant that Slovenians would never be a normal and united nation. 'About 70 years have passed since those terrible times. We are in 2012 and Slovenia is different today. Or is it really? No, alas it isn't so. The people who at that time were allowed to create terror and genocide on their own nation are still here. They live among us. With other names and surnames, but with the same identical mentality and ideology. They still always act from a position of force. They are extremely haughty and arrogant.'[23]

---

19 Of particular note are the campaigns of vilification against the president of the Association of Slovenian Writers Veno Taufer (2012) and of the eminent jurist Ljubo Bavcon, who was engaged in the civil rights movement between the 1970s and the beginning of 2013. Both noteworthy personalities were disqualified by means of deliberate factual alteration of the documents. On the manipulative use of secret service sources, see Gorazd Bajc, "Nekritična uporaba varljivih virov lahko vodi v ustvarjanje novih krivic," *Primorski dnevnik*, 24 September 2017, 13.
20 Slovenska demokratska stranka (Slovenian Democratic Party) was formed as Socialdemokratska zveza Slovenije (SDZS) on 16 February 1989. Its name was changed to Socialdemokratska stranka Slovenije (SDSS) in the same year. It has been led by Janez Janša since 1993.
21 A site near Celje where the German authorities opened a military camp was later transformed into a prison camp. In May 1945 the camp was set aside for fleeing civilians and members of the collaborating forces of various nationalities (Slovenes, Croats, Serbs, Russians, Greeks and Albanians). Germans from Kočevje, ex-members of the Kulturbund and Styrian Germans, members of the Steirischer Heimatbund, were subsequently interned. At the end of May, the *domobranci* consigned to Yugoslavia by the Anglo-American forces in Carinthia arrived. They were all executed at Bukovžlak near Teharje. A park of remembrance was inaugurated on 10 October 2004 and became a state cultural monument. See http://www.mp.gov.si/fileadmin/mp.gov.si/pageuploads/mp.gov.si/PDF/poprava_krivic/Dokumenti_in_pri cevanja_II_Teharje.pdf.
22 http://www.zaveza.si.
23 http://www.zaveza.si/index.php/component/content/article/53-teharje-2012/240-nagovor-boštjana-zadnikarja.

The battle joined in Slovenian society between opposing memories, between the heirs of the defeated and those of the victors, has a typically political background in which it is not difficult to notice a strong discord linked to the need for pre-eminence and the search for a new process of legitimisation capable of uprooting forms of continuity with the communist past and socialist society. At stake is a new society, but not only from the economic and social points of view (as has happened with neoliberal politics, for example), the distancing from a State economy and the dismantling of the social state, but also from the cultural-political point of view. A new reading of the past would confer primacy on the memories of the defeated, and renew national and political genealogy.[24] If this was to be obtained, however, a historiographical assessment was needed.

In effect, the stakes have increased in recent years and the demand for historical revision has become increasingly stronger and more radical. According to the promoters of this latest campaign, the lack of revisionist excitement demonstrated so far by large parts of Slovenian society and, moreover, the obstinate attachment to resistance values, are merely confirmation of the low level of democratisation achieved in Slovenia, the permanence of a state of political transition, and society's own incapacity to shake off the ideological legacy of the Titoist regime,[25] an incapacity determined by widespread and deeply rooted communist indoctrination.

The most direct rebuke has been directed at Slovenian academic historiography,[26] which is considered incapable of denouncing Yugoslav totalitarianism and, above all, of condemning unequivocally not only the massacres[27] that took place at the end of World War II, but also the entire experience of real socialism.[28]

In fact, the first more detailed investigations into the summary executions were carried out in the 1990s at the initiative of judicial circles ideologically close

---

24 Enzo Collotti notes how the strategy of forming a homogeneous nationalist consensus is based 'deliberately, not on a divided memory (which to be such presupposes subjects with diverse memories) but certainly on a memory cut in half, i. e. amputated of whatever does not fit the perspective of those in charge' Enzo Collotti, *Austria e non solo. Passato e presente*, XVIII (2000) 51: 6.
25 An accurate and chronological analysis is found in Peter Vodopivec, "On Slovene Troubles with the Recent Past and Historical Memory," in *Conflict and Memory: Bridging Past and Future in (South East) Europe*, edited by Wolfgang Petritsch and Vedran Džihić (Baden-Baden: Nomos, 2010), 255–256.
26 Peter Vodopivec, "L'Historiographie en Slovénie dans les années 80," in *Histoire et pouvoir en Europe médiane*, edited by Antoine Marès (Paris-Montréal: L'Hartmann, 1996), 137; Peter Vodopivec, "Zgodovine še ni konec, le spomin je kratek," *Nova revija*, 134/135 (1993): 132.
27 The *domobranci*, militants in the Slovenian collaborationist unit consigned by the British to the Yugoslav authorities in 1945, were killed *en masse* in the area of Celje and Kočevski Rog. Although exact figures are unavailable, it is estimated that there were around 13,100 members of the military and civilian anti-partisan forces.
28 Vodopivec, "On Slovene Troubles," 258–259.

to the political forces of the centre-right.[29] The lack of historiographical initiative on this theme had led to a heated debate, and subsequently made a strong political instrumentalisation of the subject possible – a process that continues today despite research having commenced, and also despite the exhumation of the remains of victims of the post-war massacres from the various mass graves spread around Slovenia.

It is important to note at this juncture that the subject of the massacres of the *domobranci*[30] was publicly confronted for the first time in Slovenia in the 1970s at the initiative of opposition-linked intellectuals, and it remained at the centre of public attention throughout the 1980s. The demand, at the time supported above all by sociologist Spomenka Hribar,[31] was for the illegitimate use of violence used by the partisan authorities at the end of the war to be acknowledged. There was considerable hostility to such requirements by a stubborn Yugoslav government. The climate was to change, however, after Slovenian independence in 1991.

During the ceremony of remembrance that took place on 8 July 1990 in Kočevski Rog, stronghold of the partisan movement and one of the sites of mass elimination of the *domobranci*, the two political sides who were to grant each other reciprocal forgiveness[32] were represented by the Slovenian president at the time, Milan Kučan, previously the reformist head of the Communist League of Yugoslavia, and by Alojzij Šuštar, Archbishop and Metropolitan of Ljubljana. On that occasion, the state accepted blame for the massacres committed by the Slovenian partisans, while the Church abstained from recognising its own responsibilities concerning its collaborationist errors. As Igor Pribac makes clear, in the years that followed, the Church preferred to assume a position of moral authority *super partes:* 'the demonstration of atonement organized near Kočevski rog should be seen as a celebration at which political heirs of the communist partisans recognized their sins and repented them, as the choice of the site itself demonstrates, while the Church gave them its absolution and

---

29 Höpken, "Tra politica della memoria e lutto," cit. 7; Lovro Šturm (ed.), *Brez milosti. Ranjeni, invalidni in bolni povojni ujetniki na Slovenskem* (Ljubljana: Nova revija, 2000).
30 *Domobranci* ("Home Guard") were established by Germans in spring of 1944 as a local branch of Wermacht. Most of the members of the Home Guard units were previously members *of Milizia Volontaria Anticommunista*, established by the Italian occupation headquarters in Ljubljana. Domobranci were armed, payed and lead by Wermacht officers.
31 After the interview by the writer Edvard Kocbek on the massacres of the *domobranci* published in Trieste in 1976 by Boris Pahor and Alojz Rebula, both Slovenian writers based in Trieste, it was Spomenka Hribar (*Krivda in greh*; Maribor: Obzorja, 1990) who demanded a proper burial for all victims of World War II.
32 On the problem of forgiveness and how one can be forgiven if the forgiveness is explicitly demanded, cf. Jacques Derrida, *Perdonare* (Milano: Raffaelo Cortina Editore, 2004), 38–39. On the theme of anger, clemency and forgiveness, see the seminal work of Martha C. Nussbaum, *Anger and Forgiveness: Resentment, Generosity, and Justice* (Oxford-New York: Oxford University Press, 2016).

imposed as a penitence the task of producing a remedy as far as humanly possible. There was a complete lack of reciprocity in the act of expiation.'[33]

The position taken by the Slovenian Church and by the forces within it, and its reading of the events of the war and the post-war period, remained decisive throughout the 1990s – and continue to be so even into the new millennium. According to the thesis propagated by the Church hierarchy, it would have been better (and certainly more convenient) for the Slovenian people to have submitted passively to the German occupation and not to have opposed the occupier.[34] In that event, they argue, there would have been fewer Slovenian casualties. In this version, the blame for the violence that occurred on Slovenian territory during and after the war falls completely on the communist-led partisan movement. Throughout the 1990s, the commitment of the Slovenian Church to the rehabilitation of collaborationism from the moral and political points of view became increasingly clear and explicit, as did the interpretation of *domobranci* as defenders of the Slovenian homeland and people against partisan barbarism and the threat of communist revolution; this commitment has also been particularly noticeable in the last 15 years. The support given by the Slovenian ecclesiastical hierarchy to the occupying forces, first Italian and then German, leading to the solemn swearing of an oath to Adolf Hitler by a unit of *domobranci* in the presence of Bishop Gregorij Rožman in the centre of Ljubljana in 1944, is understood and explained as a choice dictated exclusively by patriotic interests.[35] The political forces of the centre-right, particularly the SDS, have signalled their full agreement with the ecclesiastical thesis. They consider themselves to be the moral heirs to the defeated, pleading the cause of self-absolution from Slovenian collaborationism and presenting the *domobranci* as a patriotic, anti-communist movement. The image put forward today of the *domobranci* has become that of good men moved by a wish to preserve the honour of the homeland and the dignity of man, rather than that of a collaborationist unit active alongside Nazi and Fascist armies.[36] This image has now become widespread, and is diffused by state media in its attempt to present a balanced view on the subject of Slovenia's recent past. The declared intention of *Pričevalci*[37] ('Witnesses'), a televised series of interviews that began in 2014, was initially 'to recount the stories' of people

---

33 Igor Pribac, "Reflexionen, Erinnerungen und Bilder aus Slowenien," in *Das Unheimliche in der Geschichte. Die Foibe: Beiträge zur Psychopathologie historischer Rezeption. Die Foibe*, edited by Lusia Accati and Renate Cogoy (Berlin: Trafo, 2007), 77–104.
34 Cf. Traverso, *A ferro e a fuoco*, cit. 14.
35 France Martin Dolinar and Tamara Griesser Pečar, *Rožmanov proces* (Ljubljana: Družina, 1996).
36 Such theses are also promoted by the historian Tamara Griesser Pečar, *Razdvojeni narod: Slovenija 1941–1945: okupacija, kolaboracija, državljanska vojna, revolucija* (Ljubljana: Mladinska knjiga, 2007).
37 https://www.rtvslo.si/pricevalci.

who had not had a voice under the past regime; through selective choice of witnesses and by explicit wish of the author, Jože Možina, to rewrite history, this intention was later changed to that of clearing the collaborating forces of blame and denouncing the brutality of the partisans and communists. In 2016, for the purposes of balance, state television broadcasted a second series, *Spomini*[38] ('Memories'), directed by Janez Lombergar, which offered interviews with anti-fascist intellectuals and politicians with a background in partisan militancy. According to those at the top, placing these opposing memories alongside each other would give the Slovenian public a chance to obtain the 'historical truth' of the country's recent past.[39]

In reality, this public competition between the two narratives, anti-fascist and anti-communist, was only apparently balanced. The commitment of the political forces that understood the importance of the anti-fascist choice and of the fight for liberation was not as univocal or as organised as their opponent's.[40] It should be stressed that from the 1990s onward, the parties of the centre-left, considered by the forces of the centre-right to be unequivocal representatives of the previous regime, also made adjustments to World War II memories, keeping their distance from every meaningful connection to the previous regime. On the one hand, they laid claim to the positive actions of the anti-fascist resistance and to the emancipatory actions of the *Osvobodilna fronta*, the Slovenian liberation movement; on the other, they decried the bullying carried out by the Slovenian communist party in order to become the dominating force of the liberation movement. Their principal intention became to preserve the resistance as a founding act of independent Slovenia, thereby distancing themselves from the acts of usurpation committed by the communists, those bearers of unjust political choices. In this way, they transferred the moral burden of the post-war massacres and crimes on to the communist governing class of the time, making their revolutionary demands a culpable act.[41]

However, the Right was not satisfied with the Left merely keeping its distance from past crimes or even recanting communist ideology; rather, the objective of

---

38 https://www.rtvslo.si/oddaja/spomini/173250691.
39 For more on the debate, see https://www.mladina.si/186693/na-javni-televiziji-bi-se-mora lo-marsikaj-spremeniti; https://www.domovina.je/repe-in-pirjevec-obracunala-z-dezma nom-ne-pa-z-njegovimi-argumenti-ta-jima-predlaga-naj-se-spravita-z-resnico.
40 See the documentaries *Zločin, ki ne zastara* (2001) http://tvslo.si/predvajaj/zlocin-ki-ne-zastara/ava2.86506550; *Zamolčani – moč preživetja* (2007) http://www.rtvslo.si/odprtikop/dokumentarci/zamolcani-moc-prezivetja; Otroci s Petričkega (2007) http://www.rtvslo.si/odprtikop/dokumentarci/otroci-s-petricka.
41 Peter Vodopivec, "The Conflicting Politics of History and Memory in Slovenia since 1990," *Slovene Studies, Journal of the Society for Slovene Studies*, 1–2 (2015): 59. See also Janvit Golob, Peter Vodopivec, Tine Hribar, Janko Prunk, and Milena Basta (eds.), *Žrtve vojne in revolucije* (Ljubljana: Državni svet Republike Slovenije, 2005).

the radical rereading of Slovenia's recent past was the overturning of political relations and the repositioning of the Slovenian political axis to the right. This had come about in part, but not so far as to guarantee a lasting centre-right government. For these reasons, right-wing media campaigns after the end of the Janša government (2004–2008) focused not only on an assessment of the war and the post-war period, but also of those who had not fallen in line with the new pro-collaborationist and anti-communist narrative. The attempted burning of the biography of Milan Kučan, the first president of independent Slovenia, written by historian Božo Repe in December 2015, is an eloquent example of the climate of intolerance and hate that had developed around the political use of history. Along with Repe, lecturer in contemporary Slovenian history at Ljubljana university's history department and author of numerous studies on 20th century Slovenia, the Trieste-based historian Jože Pirjevec, an eminent scholar of Yugoslav and Slovenian history, also became one of the favourite targets of campaigns orchestrated against 'pro-partisan' and 'Bolshevik' historiography. Both were accused of politically manipulative and exploitative readings.

In the Slovenian historiographical context, the lack of historical studies on certain subjects until the end of the 1990s (subjects such as the Tito era, the relationship between society and the state in socialist Yugoslavia, and the measure of dissent generated or induced by the communist regime) is certainly significant. Moreover, there was a lack of any thorough investigation into Slovenia's contribution to the creation of socialist Yugoslavia, in particular that of Edvard Kardelj, to all intents and purposes one of the principal fathers and architects of socialist Yugoslavia and its self-management system. Such failings, which began to be overcome only as the new millennium got underway, favoured the dissemination of a distinctly anti-communist doctrine interested in presenting the populace as innocent victims of a violent communist minority; they also helped large segments of Slovenian society to suspend memory about historical events fundamental for an understanding of our own times. That said, in a forgetful society like Slovenia's, the suspension of collective memory concerning themes and questions closely linked to it is nothing new. Cases of general 'forgetfulness' were common after the dissolution of the Habsburg monarchy and the incorporation of Central Slovenia, Southern Styria, and part of Carinthia into the State of Slovenes, Croats and Serbs.[42] The same happened after 1945 and, to a similar extent, after 1991, when the continuation of any cultural links with the

---

42 On forgetfulness concerning the Austrian and German world, see Marta Verginella, "Between rejection and affinity: Slovene-German relations on the periphery of the Habsburg monarchy," in *'Die Deutschen' als die Anderen – Deutschland in der Imagination seiner Nachbarn* (= *Tel Aviver Jahrbuch für deutsche Geschichte, Vol. 40)* (Göttingen: Wallstein Verlag, 2012): 44–59.

ex-Yugoslav world was already being criticised as 'Yugo-nostalgia' and considered as proof of a lack of love for the homeland.

The lack of historiographical investigations across the board, particularly in the 1990s, opened up spaces for monolithic analysis of the communist past and for the indiscriminate use of the concept of totalitarianism. The foundations were created for a narrative in which Slovenian society was presented as an inert victim for a full 45 years (from 1945 to 1990) of power mechanisms and totalitarian state violence, and of a communist and Yugoslav system of subjection that, through top-down control along with the system of self-management, had managed to create the illusion of democracy.[43]

In the Slovenian case as well, we find ourselves faced with the inability to accept a plural and critical memory and the search of an 'overall innocence' that inserts itself so well into Central and East European mythology, permitting an explanation for the tragedies that occurred by reference to the pressure exerted by neighbours or the wickedness of others.[44] That excess of memory continues to be produced. According to Paul Ricoeur, it reinforces the position of the victim[45] and, at the same time, causes a historiographical deficit that prevents us from acquiring a more critical vision of the past.

Divided witnesses and memories

If we think of memory as a 'battlefield' (a definition proposed by Luisa Passerini in her *Utopia and Memory*),[46] then we can also agree that in the Slovenian political and social situation of the 1990s, the act of having to remember brought with it a very real proliferation of memories; and while this multiplied the use of

---

43 For thorough comprehension of what has been the communist phenomenon, is according to Claude Lefort necessary to analyse the interweaving of the political, social, economic juridical and of facts that reveal behaviours and mentalities comes apart. When attention is centred only on the regime, the society along with social structures and its transformations are not sufficiently examined thus producing in some ways an idealist history, as if the regime could function without society (Claude Lefort, "Communisme et totalitarisme," *Filozofski vestnik*, XXI (2000) 2: 11). Paul Ricoeur, *La mémoire, l'histoire, l'oubli* (Paris: Seuil, 2000, 97–105, esp. 104).

44 Peter Hanák, "Il contributo degli storici ungheresi alla trasformazione democratica," in *I muri della storia. Storici e storiografia dalle dittature alle democrazie 1945–1990*, edited by Gustavo Corni (Trieste: Lint, 1996), 207.

45 Paul Ricoeur, *La mémoire, l'histoire, l'oubli* (Paris: Seuil, 2000), 97–105 (esp. p. 104). On the temptation to transform the whole of society into a victim and the incapacity of oblivion to reconstruct an acceptable identity, see Lucette Valensi, *Fables de la mémoire* (Paris: Seuil, 1992), 12.

46 Luisa Passerini, *Memoria e utopia* (Torino: Bollati Boringhieri, 2003), 29.

memories, it also increased the instances of abuse.[47] Along with monuments to partisans and to the victors of World War II erected in the post-war period, other monuments and headstones have appeared, dedicated to the victims of the struggle for liberation and of revolutionary power. Representatives of the *Zveza borcev*, the association of partisan combatants, parade with their insignia in front of the former, while militants of the *Nova slovenska zaveza* (New Slovenian Commitment), an association committed to redeeming Slovenia from its communist past and to reassessing the patriotic commitment of the *domobranci* (as well as that of the *belogardisti* ("White Guard") and the Chetniks, i.e. all components of Slovenian collaborationism), gather in front of the latter.

Veterans of the two sides, opponents during World War II, and their supporters today raise their standards in homage to the memories on the occasion of anniversaries; they do the same for documentaries and educational TV broadcasts dedicated to the massacres and to more recent Slovenian political history, as well as at exhibitions examining the most pressing issues of World War II. It is the old and new guardians of opposing memories who inflame the debate on Slovenia's recent past in the mass media and on internet forums.

Faced with these clashes, which involve individual and collective memories, the reaction of historiography is far from unanimous. At times it intervenes and takes sides, but more often it distances itself, preferring to demonstrate its lack of connection to ideological battles fought in the name of historical truth. A further reason for this is that Slovenian historiographical circles have long set themselves against oral testimony and, in some ways, against autobiographical sources as well, thus rendering themselves incapable of methodologically and epistemologically coping with the extension of the 'frameworks' of memory and at the same time, with historical events being made instrumental to politics to such a great extent; this approach also fails to document how human memory is inevitably partial and incomplete (although this does not prevent it from being self-sufficient). As Krzysztof Pomian writes: 'As long as one remains in the area of memory, a listener who has no personal memory of what is told to him cannot do other than believe the word of the speaker who states that he is telling him what he has perceived. Memory does not manage the evidence: it is itself the evidence.'[48]

This reluctance on the part of Slovenian historiography to deal with and investigate autobiographical and oral sources precedes the so-called 'era of the witness' and has its origins in a historicistically and historiographically conservative formulation that believes that archived sources alone can serve as the foundation of historical investigation. The primacy of the written document and

---

47 Ricoeur, *La mémoire, l'histoire, l'oubli*, cit., 68.
48 Krzysztof Pomian, *Che cos'è la storia* (Milano: Bruno Mondadori, 2001), 189.

of institutional provenance has, for a long time, directed historiographical investigations and interests in Slovenia, determining not least the study of World War II. It is no coincidence that one of the rare studies of the 1990s to deal with divisions in Slovenian memories of World War II, *Rdeče in črno* ('Red and Black'), was written by two sociologists, Gregor Tomc and Doroteja Lešnik,[49] and that the ways in which war impacted on daily life in single regional situations, such as those of Carinthia and Istria, were investigated first by anthropologists and only recently by historians.[50]

In conclusion, new memories continue to proliferate in Slovenian society alongside the new and existing forms of reticence that have tended to be preserved, particularly if they have a positive value for the political framework of the moment. The exercise of memory both in its individual and collective forms remains closely linked to the identity of the single political, social, cultural subject, whether of the individual or collective kind. Revisionist talk, strongly instrumental to politics, feeds on memory, putting the absolute authenticity of the witness before a critical approach towards the evidence[51] and disregarding the fact that memory and history share the same desire to be faithful to the past (but also that they take different routes at the moment in which they have access to it). Besides being selective, memory is also strongly egocentric: it is organised around the 'I' in the first person or the 'We' in its collective version. A critical examination of sources and of the many testimonies to the past are not part of their objectives. Unlike historical knowledge, neither in its individual nor its collective form does the exercise of memory generally envision critical judgement or the necessity of integrating the 'I' or the 'We' with the memory of the other or others.

However, in an analysis of this Slovenian memorial 'battlefield',[52] it is not merely a matter of putting 200 plaques commemorating the victims of partisan and communist violence in front of hundreds of partisan monuments and monuments.[53] The stakes are higher than that. Failing to draw a distinction

---

49 Dora Lešnik and Gregor Tomc, "*Rdeče in črno. Slovensko partizanstvo in domobranstvo*" (Ljubljana: Znanstveno in publicistično središče, 1995).
50 See Gašper Mithans, "Vžgano v spominih", http://burntinmemories.eu/s1kontakt. Furthermore, one of the most interesting monographs on the Slovenian war scene was based on the skilful interweaving of oral and archive sources, and written in a microhistorical key, by eminent modernist and scholarly historian of economic history, Ferdo Gestrin, at the end of his academic career in 1991 (Ferdo Gestrin, *Svet pod Krimom v letih 1941–1942* (Ljubljana: SAZU, 1991).
51 Passerini, *Memoria e utopia*, 29.
52 On the concept of the memorial 'battlefield', see: Christopher R. Browning, *Lo storico e il testimone. Il campo di lavoro do Starachowiche* (Bari-Rome: Laterza, 2011), XV–XVI.
53 One of the few critical analyses is found in: Oto Luthar, "Preimenovanje in izključevanje kot sestavni del postkomunistične kulture spomina v Sloveniji," *Prispevki za novejšo zgodovino*, LIV-2 (2014): 195–211.

between the executioners who collaborated with the Nazi and Fascist occupiers and the victims signals a desire to close the disputes on the past. In the revisionist narrative, collaborationism becomes the consequence of communist cruelty, and its origins are explained exclusively as a reaction to communist barbarity. From this follows the notion that collaborators were victims and that the blame lies with the partisan movement *tout court*.

In the memorial inscription at Grahovo, where a recently built monument was dedicated to the victims of partisan violence, one can recognise an increasingly prominent new element in this memorial to war.[54] The executioners, defined as 'bloody brothers', are nevertheless considered to be 'foreigners in thought' and therefore harmful to the Slovenian society. The demand for their exclusion and for the denial and forgetting of their memory, which has allegedly been 'alien' to the Slovenian nation, is becoming increasingly eloquent. The claims of the defeated and their heirs do not pursue an inclusive memory of their dramas and of the tragedies suffered, but tend to formulate an exclusive and vengeful memory. For this reason, even an intense devotional attitude concerning the victims of partisan and communist violence on the part of someone who nevertheless holds anti-fascist views is not accepted as being sufficient to resolve the matter.

This was highlighted by Spomenka Hribar, for ten years a committed supporter of reconciliation between the two sides, in her comments on the monumental project supported by current Slovenian president Borut Pahor and unveiled on 13 July 2017 in Kongresni trg (Congress Square) in Ljubljana. The monument is meant to render justice to all Slovenian victims of all wars. But while it serves to render all violence equal, it also makes revolution a crime – and counter-revolution a legitimate choice.[55]

At the same time, the form of the monument reproduces current political divisions, chooses the paradigm of the Slovenian Second World War to represent the deaths that occurred in other wars as well.[56] It is without a doubt symptomatic that the symbolic value of a monument that should have rendered justice to all victims of all wars, and therefore served as a symbol of Slovenian reconciliation, was disavowed even before its construction.

---

54 Pascal Blanchard and Isabelle Veyrat-Masson, *Les guerres de mémoires. La France et son histoire* (Paris: La Découverte, 2010; 1st ed. 2008).
55 Spomenka Hribar, "Spomini, ki družijo, spomini, ki ločujejo," *Mladina* 34 (21 August 2015): 20–24.
56 https://www.delo.si/sobotna/spomenik-ki-bo-zapicen-v-nase-osrcje-za-vselej.html; https://en.wikipedia.org/wiki/Monument_to_the_Victims_of_All_Wars.

Bojan Godeša

Slovenian Historiography in the Grip of Reconciliation

This paper sheds light on the clarification of the past considered to be controversial (particularly the period of the 1941–1945 occupation), through the prism of national reconciliation. In Slovenian society, there exist very different evaluations of the engagement of Slovenian political subjects in World War II. This issue has marked Slovenian society for the last thirty years, and its impacts are still felt today.

Given the fact that a biased image of World War II prevailed in Slovenia for a long time, it is clear that this image had to be modernized from the point of view of interpretation, and a balance between the two opposing interpretations had to be found. Although entirely legitimate in its essence, the demand for such clarification of the past has not predominantly developed into a constructive dialogue characterized by an unbiased, academically or scientifically impeccable approach aiming for comprehensive reflection on the wartime events. What came to the fore was a struggle for interpretive supremacy largely characterized by a "myth-against-myth" principle. In such an atmosphere, scientific principles do not always form the basis of an exclusively methodological approach to the wartime past. Within such a context, this paper largely focuses on the presentation of a methodological and ideological model, with which part of the Slovene historiography has been trying to rehabilitate the Slovenian political camp – tarnished with collaboration and defeated in 1945 – by promoting the slogan "no truth, no reconciliation."

In Yugoslav society, the idea of the necessity for national reconciliation emerged in the context of general ideological relief during the aftermath of Tito's death in 1980, with Serbia and Slovenia being the first two republics to champion such reconciliation. In Slovenia, the issue of national reconciliation became a relevant question largely due to the work of Spomenka Hribar, whose essay "Krivda in greh" ("Guilt and Sin") defined the need for national reconciliation, and called for the erection of a monument to all victims of World War II. Hribar's essay was published in a collection of papers dedicated to Edvard Kocbek, which was put together in 1984, but was not published until 1987.¹ Nevertheless, its contents were well known, as they circulated among a sub-section of the general public.

Hribar's proposal sparked fierce controversy, with responses ranging from support to complete rejection. Despite media confrontations, which in 1985 culminated in the expulsion of Spomenka Hribar from the League of Communists, over the following years the issue of national reconciliation affirmed itself as a legitimate topic among the general Slovenian public. In the second half of the 1980s, when Slovenia was strengthening its desire to secure an independent position for itself within the Yugoslav state, the idea of national reconciliation provided an appropriate basis for overcoming internal differences and attaining unity, which was necessary for the realization of Slovenia's basic objective.²

Spomenka Hribar's views echoed strongly not only at home, but also among Slovenian political émigrés. The majority of such representatives complimented her on her courage for having publicly addressed the question of the post-war massacres of 1945, an issue constantly present in Slovenian society. The first news about the massacres leaked out during their immediate aftermath; later on, however, people would only whisper about them, as no one dared to speak about them publicly. This silence was only broken in 1975, when the Trieste literary magazine *Zaliv* published Boris Pahor and Alojz Rebula's interview with Edvard Kocbek. Kocbek, a representative of the Catholic group in the Liberation Front, and one of the main figures of the Slovenian resistance, spoke out about the post-war massacres.³ Though the magazine was forbidden in Slovenia (Yugoslavia), the Slovenian authorities decided to reprint the entire interview in the most prominent Slovenian intellectual magazine, *Naši razgledi*. Concomitantly, the magazine published contributions by several members of Kocbek's wartime "comradeship"⁴ contradicting Kocbek, but they could not deny the fact that following the war the massacres did take place. As a result, after 1975 this fact was no longer a "public secret."⁵ Nevertheless, until the period of ideological relief in the mid-1980s, the situation in Slovenia did not permit serious discussion over

---

1 Spomenka Hribar, "Krivda in greh," in *Kocbekov zbornik,* edited by Dimitrij Rupel (Maribor: Obzorja, 1987), 6–68.
2 Sašo Cmrečnjak, "Slovenska sprava: zgodovinski pregled" *Zgodovinski časopis*, 70 (2016) 3–4: 16–19; Bojan Godeša, "Reconciliation instead of History," *Quarter of a Century of the Republic of Slovenia: Prispevki za novejšo zgodovino*, 56 (2016) 3: 101–117.
3 Boris Pahor has recently re-addressed the issue in a book published in September 2018. Boris Pahor, Peter Kovačič Peršin and Mihael Glavan, *Brez Kocbekovega sodelovanja ne bi bilo Osvobodilne fronte* (Ljubljana: Cankarjeva založba, 2018).
4 *Tovarišija*, the title of Kocbek's war diary, published in 1949. Edvard Kocbek, *Tovarišija. Dnevniški zapiski od 17. maja 1942 do 1. maja 1943* (Ljubljana: Državna založba Slovenije, 1949).
5 Igor Omerza, *Edvard Kocbek. Osebni dosje št. 584* (Ljubljana: Karantanija, 2010).

the issue. Such discussion was spurred only by the publication of Nikolai Tolstoy's book *The Minister and the Massacres* in 1986, and Anthony Cowgill's Commission Report.[6] International attention paid to the issue gave rise to an intense scholarly debate in the Slovenian press (i. e. in the magazine *Naši razgledi*, and the Saturday supplement of the daily newspaper *Delo*), which published contributions by Robert Knight, Dušan Biber and Dušan Nećak.[7]

Increasingly prominent in Slovenian society since the mid-1980s, the issue of national reconciliation culminated in the commemoration that took place in the Kočevje Rog forest in July 1990. It was attended by the highest representatives of political and public life, including the President of the Presidency of the Republic of Slovenia, Milan Kučan, and the Ljubljana Archbishop Alojzij Šuštar, who held a mass. The aim of the commemoration was to take "the first step toward appeasement, so important for the Slovenian nation and its state," and thus contribute to "the creation of such circumstances in Slovenia's political and public life in which the past will no longer be a burden on interpersonal relations."[8]

A few months before the commemoration, on 4 March 1990, just before the April elections (which were the first democratic elections in Yugoslavia after 1927), the SRS Presidency issued a "Statement on National and Civil Appeasement."[9] This statement was substantiated with the words that "in this serious and pivotal moment of the transition to a pluralist democratic system, it is obligatory to raise the question that the public views as the issue of 'national reconciliation.'"[10] According to the SRS Presidency, this issue had to be addressed in order to encourage the creation of the kind of atmosphere in Slovenia's political and public life, in which the past would no longer be a burden on today's and tomorrow's interpersonal relations. During that period, forty-five years after the

---

6 Anthony Cowgill, Christopher Booker, Lord Thomas Brimelow, and Teddy Tryon-Wilson, "Interim Report on an Enquiry into the Repatriation of Surrendered Enemy Personnel to the Soviet Union and Yugoslavia From Austria in May 1945 and the Alleged 'Klagenfurt Conspiracy'" (London, September 1988).

7 These details and information constitute a suitable addition to the dissertation by Davor Zebec (*Die Massentötungen nach Kriegsende 1945 auf dem jugoslawischen Kriegsschauplatz. Ein Vergleich der kroatischen und slowenischen Historiografie* (Thesis), University of the Federal Armed Forces Munich, Faculty of State and Social Sciences, Neubiberg, 2017), in which such elements concerning "prehistory" are not included.

8 Božo Repe, *Viri o demokratizaciji in osamosvojitvi Slovenije. 2. del. – Slovenci in federacija* (Ljubljana: Arhivsko društvo Slovenije, 2003), 21.

9 The wording of the statement was written on the basis of the draft prepared by the historian Janko Pleterski, who was a member of the Presidency of the Socialist Republic of Slovenia (1988–1990). Later on, Janko Pleterski explained his attitude toward reconciliation in the article "O NOB in spravi," published in: *Narodnoosvobodilni boj v slovenskem narodnem spominu : Slovenski zbornik 2007*, edited by Janez Stanovnik et al, GO ZZB NOB Slovenije, Ljubljana, 2007, 23–31.

10 "Narodna umiritev kot pogoj za mirno sožitje," *Delo* 32, no. 54 (5 March 1990): 1–2.

end of the war, the problem of national and civil appeasement remained present. It is in the interest of public well-being that national politics should aim to eliminate any possibility of a civil split.[11] Having brought the issue up to the level of state institutions, the Statement of the SRS Presidency marked a turning point in the attitude taken toward reconciliation processes. All previous reconciliation proposals had been put forward exclusively by civil society.

A few days after the Statement of the SRS Presidency, yet still prior to the April elections, the Slovenian Regional Episcopal Conference released a "Statement on National Reconciliation" at its session on March 13.[12] In the introduction, the statement welcomed the gesture of the SRS Presidency as an important step toward "finding a solution to this vital issue and the future of the Slovenian nation." However, the conference found it important to emphasize that "our statement does not want to comment on individual claims of the Statement of the SRS Presidency. That should be undertaken through a public discussion."[13] The statement went on to say the following:

> According to the Slovenian Regional Episcopal Conference, the Church shall pursue appeasement as its primary goal to the best of its ability, and it wishes to cooperate honestly with everyone who holds this goal dear. Appeasement, however, cannot be ordered or forced. The only path toward this goal is reconciliation; otherwise there can be no permanent and true appeasement. The first and foremost task is therefore to attain reconciliation. [...] As far as this is concerned, we should first take into account reconciliation with the dead, and then reconciliation with the living. The latter cannot be attained without the former. [...] In order to ensure reconciliation among the living, which is the only path to national appeasement, we believe we should [...] establish the full and comprehensive historical truth about all events that took place from the beginning of the last war until today. Only truth can set us free and serve as the basis for reconciliation, thus paving the way for appeasement. Thus, the primary task is to objectively ascertain and publish all facts, in so far as that is possible, based on documents and testimonies. The unresolved past cannot simply be forgotten or erased, especially because so far so many untruths have been disseminated; nor has it been possible to ascertain and reveal the truth at all.[14]

---

11 Ibid.
12 France Martin Dolinar, "Resnici na ljubo. Izjave ljubljanskih škofov o medvojnih dogodkih," *Družina*, (Ljubljana, 1998): 31–34.
13 Ibid. An extensive public discussion did indeed take place. Boris Mlakar prepared the introductory questions for the survey entitled "National Reconciliation – The End of the Civil War?", which turned out to be one of the most resonant surveys at the time: *Borec. Revija za zgodovino, antropologijo in književnost*, 5–6–7 (1990): 582–716.
14 Dolinar, "Resnici na ljubo," 31–34.

As mentioned, the ceremony of reconciliation – first proposed by Spomenka Hribar[15] – was held in the Kočevje Rog forest. Its concept – a state and Church event including a religious ceremony and two speeches (by the President of the Presidency of the Republic of Slovenia, and by the Slovenian Metropolitan)[16] – was drawn up by the Presidency of the Republic of Slovenia (hereon: the RS Presidency) that had been democratically elected in the April elections.

On 2 July 1990, shortly before the ceremony, the Justice and Peace Commission operating under the auspices of the Slovenian Regional Episcopal Conference released a statement entitled "For a Deeper Understanding of Reconciliation," signed by its then President Anton Stres, who was later the Bishop of Celje (2006–2009) and then the Archbishop of Ljubljana (2010–2014). The statement expressed the expectations of the Roman Catholic Church in Slovenia as regards reconciliation far more directly:

> Prior to the funeral ceremony dedicated to the people killed in the Kočevje Rog Forest, our community as well as the emigrant public still strongly fosters numerous and sometimes very diverse attitudes toward the so-called reconciliation. There are many misunderstandings and inaccurate assessments of the intentions of both parties. Therefore, it is appropriate that we once again clarify the purpose of the funeral ceremony in Kočevje Rog, and explain its connection with reconciliation, which will undoubtedly be a long process. The Kočevje Rog Forest is the resting place of those killed who the winners of the war simply wanted to erase from our memory. The aim of the funeral ceremony is to restore them the most basic human dignity we owe to the dead: to be counted among the dead and to have one's own grave. [...] We are well aware of the fact that this does not conclude, but merely begins, the process of reconciliation. Reconciliation cannot be attained without the truth, one that is as thorough as possible, and the path toward such truth is still a long one. We will only be able to reach it if we overcome a variety of preconceptions, especially those stemming from our different ideologies. [...] Therefore, we cannot agree with those who argue that the past should simply be forgotten. That would mean that we just want to patch up, rather than heal, the wound. Even worse: it would mean that the injustice should be left uncorrected – which is the same as agreeing to it. It is clear, naturally, that it will not be possible to completely right all the wrongs. That, however, does not morally exempt us from trying to do at least what can be done.[17]

Having expressed its official standpoint, the Catholic Church in Slovenia joined the reconciliation efforts, and took on the role of advocate for the interests of those whose victimhood had been kept a secret. It attempted to assert itself as an

---

15 Zdenko Roter, *Padle maske. Od partizanskih sanj do novih dni* (Ljubljana: Sever & Sever, 2013), 412–413.
16 Božo Repe, *Milan Kučan, prvi predsednik* (Ljubljana: Modrijan, 2015), 282–283.
17 "Za globlje razumevanje sprave. Izjava komisije Pravičnost in mir (Prof Anton Stres)," *Družina* (8 July 1990): 13.

equal partner of the state, and partly as the only true representative of the Slovenian nation – or at least as its supreme moral authority.

As for the political émigrés in exile, individual emigrants (e. g. Vinko Levstik, Ciril Žebot, Branko Rozman) sporadically expressed their desire for reconciliation as early as in the 1960s. Later on, the political émigrés participated in the making of the homeland, mostly through the Slovenian World Congress established at its constitutive meeting on June 27 and 28, 1991 in Ljubljana. It was envisioned as an "all-Slovenian organization connecting and uniting Slovenes at home and abroad on the basis of their commitment to Sloveneness, irrespective of their ideological, political and other differences."[18] The issue of national reconciliation was at the centre of the organization's attention, since its establishment was listed as one of the main goals in its statute.[19] National reconciliation was also at the forefront of public attention in 1990. Over the following months, it became less prominent as the general public was more focused on attaining independence.

Symbolically, the reconciliation efforts bore fruit in the summer of 2017 when the Monument to the Victims of All Wars and war-related victims in the territory of the Republic of Slovenia was unveiled. Its erection was regarded as the realization of long-standing aspirations to attain national reconciliation, and a (very belated) reply to Spomenka Hribar's call for the building of a monument in Ljubljana dedicated to all those who "died for the motherland," expressed in her essay "Krivda in greh." It was also supposed to symbolize the key step toward final reconciliation among Slovenes. A visit to the monument came to be included in the state protocol observed during the official visits of foreign guests.

The monument was officially unveiled on 13 July 2017, and the keynote speech was given by Borut Pahor, the President of the Republic of Slovenia. He has been an avid supporter of reconciliation: he was the introductory speaker at the international conference "Confronting the Past: Challenges of the Process of Reconciliation in Slovenia," organized under his patronage by the Museum of Contemporary History of Slovenia and the Friedrich Ebert Foundation.[20] On that occasion, he expressed his belief that "Slovenia is founded on reconciliation," and concluded his speech by pointing out: "When we talk about reconciliation,

---

18 *Gradivo otvoritvenega zasedanja Svetovnega slovenskega kongresa, Ljubljana, 27. in 28. junija 1991* (Ljubljana: Svetovni slovenski kongres, Konferenca za R. Slovenijo, 1994), 3.
19 Ibid.
20 An international conference under the patronage of the President of the Republic of Slovenia Borut Pahor: "Soočanje s preteklostjo: Izzivi spravnega procesa v Sloveniji," 5 June 2017, Muzej novejše zgodovine Slovenije, Ljubljana. Organized by the Friedrich Ebert Foundation and the Museum of Contemporary History of Slovenia. Participants: Gorazd Bajc, Bojan Godeša, Tamara Griesser Pečar, Tvrtko Jakovina, Anton Jamnik, Annette Kaminsky, Andreja Valič Zver. Available at: http://www.scnr.si/sl/napovednik/vabilo-na-mednarodno-konferen co-o-spravnem-procesu-v-sloveniji.

we do not talk about the past. We talk about our future."[21] When unveiling the monument, Pahor said that Slovenia had received not only a new monument, but also a common site of memory of victims. He also emphasized the importance of shared national memories, irrespective of the different values potentially attributed to them by the population. The act of erecting such a monument made Slovenia a mature nation.[22] The ceremony ended with a prayer for the victims offered by the Ljubljana Archbishop Stanislav Zore.

Fig. 1: Monument to the Victims of All Wars, Ljubljana – Kongresni trg 2017 (© Andrej Furlan, ZRC SAZU).

At the monument's unveiling, the President of the Slovenian state expressed his general stance clearly and unambiguously. The stance of the other "partner," the Catholic Church – if the unveiling is perceived as the continuation of the process begun at the ceremony in Kočevje Rog in the summer of 1990 – was expressed in 2015 in a reply by Tadej Strehovec, Secretary of the Justice and Peace Commission. His reply was to a question posed by Ivan Puc, a journalist from the magazine *Reporter*:

---

21 President of the Republic of Slovenia: "Slovenija je utemeljena na spravi," available at http://www.up-rs.si/up-rs/uprs.nsf/objave/AD72380D65C9EA5DC1258136002F5ED2?OpenDocument.

22 Speech by the President of the Republic of Slovenia Borut Pahor at the unveiling ceremony of the Monument to the Victims of All Wars and War-related Victims, Ljubljana, 13 July 2017, available at: http://www.up-rs.si/up-rs/uprs.nsf/objave/D2FB2A48C140B6F7C125815C005D947C?OpenDocument.

The Justice and Peace Commission, operating under the auspices of the Slovenian Episcopal Conference, supports all the efforts of the national authorities and civil society organizations aimed at achieving reconciliation in Slovenian society. We believe that the erection of a monument to the victims of all wars makes sense, after a realistic evaluation of the historical situation during and after World War II, and a concrete commitment to providing a decent burial for all victims of wartime and revolutionary violence. We expect that the potential erection of such a monument will be seen as appropriate only if a consensus is reached among politicians and all major civil society organizations in this area.[23]

The ceremony was not attended by organizations representing the interests of war veterans, the Union of Associations for the Values of the National Liberation Movement of Slovenia, on the one hand, nor by the New Slovene Covenant[24] on the other. None of their activities demonstrates signs of identification with the monument and its message. There are also many other responses clearly demonstrating that the tensions between ideological opponents have not yet been overcome.

In order to understand the situation better, Jože Dežman, President of the Government Commission for the Solution of the Issue of Hidden Burial Grounds, offered the following explanation: "The monument should be the top of a pyramid that, however, does not exist. The pyramid will be built when victims' burial grounds are no longer unkempt, and a national register of victims and their burial grounds has been compiled. [...] Currently, the burial grounds of the majority of victims have not been taken care of, nor has the register of victims and their burial grounds been compiled. Therefore, we can argue that the Republic of Slovenia has not yet tried to bury all 'war victims and war-related victims'."[25] The majority of work related to the discovery of hidden burial grounds in Slovenia was undertaken by Mitja Ferenc and his team; however, their work has not yet been completed and further research is envisaged.[26] Another project that ought to be highlighted in this context is that of "Second World War Victims and War-Related Victims on the Territory of Today's Republic of Slovenia," carried out by the Institute of Contemporary History. Its team suc-

---

23 https://katoliska-cerkev.si/stalisce-kpm-o-spomeniku-zrtvam-vseh-vojn.
24 Established in May 1991, the New Slovene Covenant ("Nova Slovenska zaveza") is an organization promoting the tradition of the Slovene Covenant (established in 1942) under whose auspices the leaders of prewar parties (with the exception of the Communist Party of Slovenia) coordinated their operations during the occupation. The organization presents itself as the representative of all those entities and persons in Slovenian society holding a positive view of the acts of the prewar political elite and of the Catholic leadership during the occupation. It publishes a magazine called *Zaveza* ("Covenant").
25 Jože Dežman and Pavel Jamnik, *Slovenija in vojna grobišča. Dolga tranzicija* (Ljubljana: Komisija Vlade RS za reševanje prikritih grobišč, 2017), 10.
26 Mitja Ferenc, "Post-War Killings and Concealed Gravesites of World War II in Slovenia," *Slovene Studies. Journal of the Society for Slovene Studies,* 40 (2018) 1–2: 77–91.

ceeded in registering the majority of victims, with their number totalling almost 100,000 – which accounts for 6.7 % of the population of that time.[27]

Unfortunately, so far, reconciliation efforts have neither managed to clarify the wartime past, nor to put an end to ideological divisions.[28] It is becoming increasingly clear that they have only widened the gap in Slovenian society in terms of how it views its past (particularly the period of occupation, 1941–1945).

Different attitudes toward the issue of national reconciliation surfaced as early as in 1990, when its premises were defined. The political authorities of the time defined the entire process as a policy of appeasement, evading the term "reconciliation" in their statement, focusing on the aspect of piety (i. e. the right to a decent burial ground and public memory), and recommending that the treatment of pressing issues from the past be depoliticized,[29] while the Slovenian leadership of the Catholic Church made very resolute demands for a re-evaluation of the past, emphasizing that "only truth can set us free and serve as the basis for reconciliation, thus paving the way for appeasement."[30]

The answer to the question of how to evaluate the developments during the 1941–1945 occupation, and the acts of those directly involved in the war, lies at the heart of the whole set of issues relating to reconciliation efforts, if this notion is used as a *terminus technicus*.

An important symbolic turning point in the intensification of the ideological schism was the 50th anniversary of the end of World War II, in 1995. On that occasion, the Slovenian Episcopal Conference issued the following statement entitled "In the Service of Truth, Justice and Reconciliation":

> World War II has been etched in the memory of our nation not only as a sad period of occupation, but also as a period of profound national division and fratricidal war. This horrific wound caused by national discord has not yet healed, and even 50 years after the end of the war we are still incapable of carrying out essential acts of national reconciliation. [...] It seems that the current authorities do not show enough motivation and do not provide enough opportunities to explore our recent history and to right the injustices.[31]

The unrealized expectations of the Catholic Church in Slovenia must have begotten the belated interpretation of the 1990 ceremony in the Kočevje Rog Forest

---

27 Vida Deželak-Barič, "Posledice vojnega nasilja : smrtne žrtve druge svetovne vojne in zaradi nje na Slovenskem" in *Nasilje vojnih in povojnih dni*, edited by Nevenka Troha (Ljubljana: Inštitut za novejšo zgodovino, 2014), 11–46. Comprehensive data and the database are accessible at: http://www.sistory.si/zrtve.
28 Božo Repe, *Jutri je nov dan: Slovenci in razpad Jugoslavije* (Ljubljana: Modrijan, 2002), 127.
29 "Narodna umiritev kot pogoj," 1–2.
30 Dolinar, "Resnici na ljubo," 31–34.
31 Ibid, 34–38.

expressed in 2015 by the Ljubljana Auxiliary Bishop Anton Jamnik, on the occasion of the 70th anniversary of the end of the war:

> The event was carefully orchestrated. Throughout all these years, all sorts of media have promoted it as spin in Slovenia and abroad, thus shaping – or, to put it more succinctly, manipulating – public opinion, conveying the impression that the Kočevje Rog event was a so-called 'ceremony of reconciliation,' with Archbishop Šuštar and President Kučan acting as partners in it. Such an explanation indeed 'took root' among people, even if it was merely manipulation resulting from well-calculated pragmatism. It was a fraud that persists even today.[32]

The belief that the ceremony of reconciliation in Kočevje Rog contained "elements of deception" was also expressed by Lojze Peterle, who was the first Prime Minister of the Republic of Slovenia.[33] Revealingly, a very similar opinion was expressed by Jože Pučnik, the leader of the Democratic Opposition of Slovenia (DEMOS), the coalition that won the 1990 elections, and the first Deputy Prime Minister, at the 33rd Draga Study Days in 1998.[34]

Milan Kučan, who was President of the Presidency of the Republic of Slovenia in 1990, and later President of the Republic of Slovenia for two consecutive terms (1993–2002), expressed his opinion on the issue of reconciliation and the ceremony in Kočevje Rog in an interview:

> *How did you envision that the process of reconciliation would continue after you shook hands with Archbishop Alojzij Šuštar?*
> "I saw the reconciliatory ceremony as a pious rather than a political act. However, in Slovenia the opinion prevailed that we were dealing with a political problem in need of a political solution."
> *Was that the reason why you did not support Pahor's 1997 Resolution, written by Spomenka Hribar?*
> "In view of what I have learnt from my experience at the reconciliatory ceremony in Kočevje Rog and in view of its intentional underestimation, I was of the opinion that the situation was not yet ready for such a resolution. Generally speaking, I do not believe resolutions are the proper way of dealing with such issues. I perceive reconciliation as a sign of the maturity of the nation, of its capability of saying at a certain moment: This is our history, our past. It happened, for better or worse. We have to take it upon ourselves and live with it. There is nothing wrong with resolutions, symbols and monuments per se, but they will not produce any results by themselves. For as long as reconciliation is not in the interest of the politics of the time, it will not happen. I see reconciliation first

---

32 Anton Jamnik, "Kdor trdi, da sprava ni možna, je obupal nad človekom," *Slovenski čas* (montly supplement of *Družina*), June 2015.
33 Jernej Vrtovec, *Vloga nadškofa Šuštarja pri osamosvojitvi Slovenije* (Celje: Društvo Mohorjeva družba, Celjska Mohorjeva družba, 2016), 96.
34 Jože Pučnik, "Sprava kot izhodišče za civilno rast Slovencev iz naroda v državo," *Biti to, kar si. 33. študijski dnevi Draga 98*, edited by Sergij Pahor, Saša Martelanc and Marij Maver (Trieste: Mladika, 1999), 137–138.

and foremost as an intimate human act. I often wonder, though, whether anything can be more reconciliatory among Slovenes than the joint establishment of their own state and their current responsibility for its future. Unfortunately, Slovenian politics refused to recognize this act as an act of reconciliation. Moreover, I am convinced that what Slovenia lacks is an antifascist agreement, and this impedes reconciliation as I understand it. Current Slovenian politics is not able to reach such an agreement, hence the difficulties in defining the attitude taken toward various forms of totalitarianism."[35]

According to Božo Repe's biography of Kučan, *Milan Kučan, prvi predsednik*, "the ceremony of reconciliation was one of the most delicate and far-reaching of Kučan's acts during his first term of office."[36]

Slovenian Historiography and the Process of Reconciliation

When introducing interpretive pluralism, most Slovenian historiography has not shed light on the interpretive image of World War II. Nevertheless, over time, public discourse witnessed the first attempts to put the issues of wartime collaboration, national treason and counter-revolution under the microscope. One of the watershed moments occurred on 27 May 1985, when the Section for Historiographical Issues of the Marxist Center of the Central Committee of the League of Communists of Slovenia organized the first public round table on collaboration and national treason. The event was spurred by Boris Mlakar's article "The Twentieth Century Also Gave Birth to Collaboration," published on 4 May 1985 in the daily newspaper *Delo*.[37] In addition to Boris Mlakar, the round table saw the participation of Bogo Grafenauer, Ivan Križnar, Milan Ževart and Ljubo Bavcon; their papers were published in the journal *Teorija in praksa*.[38]

Slovenian historiography during the late 1980s and early 1990s was marked by a number of changes. It finally paid attention to the obsoleteness of patterns developed in the aftermath of World War II, and questioned not only the ideological perspective taken in historiography, but also its methodology, terminology and prioritization of topics. Owing to a more relaxed political atmosphere, it could leave behind monolithic thinking, re-evaluate one-sided perspectives imbued with ideological stereotypes, eliminate taboos and permit the existence of plural models of historical interpretation.

The post-war regime in Slovenia (Yugoslavia) (1945–1990) founded its le-

---

35 "Milan Kučan," in *Slovenija in pika!*, edited by Boštjan Furlan, Ožbej Peterle, Marko Balažic (Ljubljana: Cankarjeva založba, 2016), 209–211.
36 Repe, *Milan Kučan*, 281.
37 Mlakar, Boris. "20. stoletje je rodilo tudi kolaboracijo," *Delo*, May 4, 1985, p. 22.
38 "Kolaboracionizem, narodno izdajstvo, protirevolucija," *Teorija in praksa*, no. 9–10, 1986, 994–1015.

gitimacy upon the developments that took place during the occupation and in the immediate aftermath of the Second World War (i.e. in the so-called period of the National Liberation Struggle and People's Revolution). As a result of this, post-war historiography was largely subjugated to the regime's perspective. Those who were on the losing side of the war, along with their truths, had no right to public existence in their own motherland, nor could they participate in shaping the image of the recent past. Their views on the wartime developments could only be developed in exile, mostly in Argentina and the USA, where approximately 15,000 opponents of the Partisan movement found shelter.[39] Their interpretation, naturally, tended to provide explanations and excuses for their stance during the war and was, consequently, schematic and black-and-white.

Unsurprisingly, the new situation brought to the fore the question of balance between two interpretations diametrically opposed in terms of content. In relation to the genesis of the wartime events, they are mirror images of each other, differing only in the positive/negative connotation ascribed to the developments, rather than in the mental structure through which they view the controversial period.

Optimistic expectations that the democratization of society would put an end to political pressure on historiography have not always been met. The clarification of the developments during World War II in Slovenia remains one of the major issues in contemporary Slovenian society, and the consequences of these developments are still being felt today. The period from 1941 to 1945 remains the most disputed historical topic in Slovenia. Different political groups, everywhere, view not only the present but also the past differently, and Slovenia is no exception. In other words, the topic of World War II has become a political issue par excellence, misused by advocates of various political groups for the purpose of political strife.

In 1995, a group of historians[40] – at the request of the National Assembly of the Republic of Slovenia – even prepared a scientific report on contemporary Slovenian history (entitled "Crucial Characteristics of Slovenian Politics 1929–1955")[41] in order to provide the Assembly with the historiographical basis for dealing with open issues about the recent past. However, even after this

---

39 Vodopivec, Peter. "Populacijske posledice 2. svetovne vojne in povojnega nasilja na Slovenskem," *Žrtve vojne in revolucije : zbornik : referati in razprava s posveta v Državnem svetu 11. in 12. novembra 2004, ki sta ga pripravila Državni svet Republike Slovenije in Inštitut za novejšo zgodovino v Ljubljani,* edited by Golob, Janvit, et al., Državni svet Republike Slovenije, Ljubljana, 2005, 9599.
40 Zdenko Čepič, Tone Ferenc, Aleš Gabrič, Bojan Godeša, Boris Mlakar, Dušan Nećak, Jože Prinčič, Janko Prunk, Božo Repe, Anka Vidovič-Miklavčič, Peter Vodopivec, and Milan Ževart.
41 Zdenko Čepič et al. (eds.), *Ključne značilnosti slovenske politike v letih 1929–1955: znanstveno poročilo* (Ljubljana: Inštitut za novejšo zgodovino, 1995).

attempt to elevate the discussion from the political to the scholarly level, passions still run high when the unresolved past is at stake.

Although entirely legitimate in its essence, the demand for clarification of the past has not developed into a predominantly constructive dialogue characterized by an unbiased, academically or scientifically impeccable approach, the aim of which would be a comprehensive reflection on the wartime events. It became increasingly evident relatively early on that such a development was not likely to take place, and among the first to point out that fact were the eminent Professors Ferdo Gestrin and Bogo Grafenauer, both members of the Slovenian Academy of Sciences and Arts.[42] In watershed moments, research energy became largely focused on the political and ideological (re)interpretation of World War II, with methodological and conceptual questions being rather marginalized.[43] It has to be pointed out, though, that in the context of research into recent history in post-communist Eastern Europe, the Slovenian situation is specific rather than exceptional.[44]

Owing to the different wartime circumstances in Yugoslavia in which communists, having called for an armed struggle against the occupiers, succeeded in harmonizing national and ideological incentives with the Allies' objectives, the Slovenian territory has been marked by specific features that make it considerably different to other Eastern European countries liberated by the Red Army. The Slovenian situation is most comparable with those in the other former Yugoslav republics, which is unsurprising given their common past. Yet even within these cases, one can observe differences in the various nations' approaches to the events of World War II.[45]

The almost thirty years of the Slovenian nation-state were thus largely marked by political conflict in the domestic arena, which has become known by the more or less felicitous term "cultural struggle." It has to be pointed out that this initially brought about positive results, one of the most noticeable being the shift from a schematic and one-sided portrayal of World War II to a complex and multi-layered scrutiny of this period. As a result of such attempts to clarify the past, the interpretation of war events that had been forbidden and repressed in Slovenia – but which had remained extremely alive in exile – was finally given

---

42 Bojan Godeša, "Grafenauer in Gestrin – njuni posegi v zgodovino dvajsetega stoletja," in *O mojstrih in muzi. Zgodovinopisje Boga Grafenauerja in Ferda Gestrina*, edited by Peter Štih and Žiga Zwitter (Ljubljana: Slovenska akademija znanosti in umetnosti, 2018), 196–212.
43 Bojan Godeša, "Social and Cultural Aspects of the Historiography on the Second World War in Slovenia / Sozialgeschichte und Soziale Bewegungen in Slowenien / Social History and Social Movements in Slovenia," *Mitteilungsblatt des Instituts für soziale Bewegungen*, 41 (2009): 111–125.
44 Ibid.
45 Bojan Godeša and Boris Mlakar, "Storia della resistenza e della guerra mondiale : la Slovenia e l'ex-Jugoslavia," *Contemporanea* 9 (January 2006) 1: 123–132.

legitimacy and the right to exist. Gradually, different perspectives evolved and legitimate differences in views held by individual historians surfaced: a completely logical and normal state of affairs in democratic societies.

These changes in Slovenian historiography have raised the question of historical revisionism. While the importance of such discussions should not be disregarded, in Slovenia they – on too many occasions – turned into more or less scholastic debates. This was largely because of terminological imprecision, as well as an infinite number of interpretations of the significance of revision and revisionism. Peter Vodopivec expressed his concern for this situation, which is typical for Slovenian society as a whole (as well as internationally) in the following way: "I am afraid that what we are facing today is an ideational and political confusion."[46]

Naturally, revision by itself is not necessarily a negative phenomenon, but rather a more or less logical consequence of a new reading of the past. Views of the past are subject to change, and this phenomenon is not limited only to post-communist societies, though in their case it is perhaps more prominent owing to the depth of change. It is characteristic of history that it addresses historical topics anew, and questions established views. The writing of history entails witnessing constant changes to histories, and the emergence of new interpretations. Each generation views and questions the past from the perspective of the time in which it lives.[47]

Slovenian society has been witnessing a tendency to establish, as the only credible view of events during the occupation, an interpretation whose basic features were formed by the Partisans' opponents as early as during the war, before being elaborated upon, and adapted to new circumstances in exile, and finally being transplanted back to their motherland after the emergence of interpretive pluralism. Naturally, such an approach did not develop in order to laboriously disclose the most credible image of the past, which is supposed to be the aspiration of contemporary Slovenian historiography. Instead, it sought to ensure the dominance of their own interpretation, and thus exculpate the engagements of Slovenian anti-communists during World War II, or at least present these engagements in a more favourable light.

If one bears in mind the phenomenon of cultural struggle in Slovenia, it is unsurprising that the emigrants' interpretation has been adopted by parts of

---

46 Peter Vodopivec, "Noben narod ni rojen samo iz kulture. Slovenska zgodovina : monografija, ki velja za enega največjih sintetičnih dosežkov slovenskega zgodovinopisja," *Delo* (27 December 2016): 13.
47 Chiara Agagiù, "'Nel giardino del vicino.' Alcune considerazioni intorno alla storiografia sull'occupazione italiana in Slovenia (1941–1943)," *Eunomia. Rivista semestrale di Storia e Politica Internazionali* 5 (2016) 1: 221–252, available at: https://core.ac.uk/download/pdf/45688180.pdf.

Slovenian historiography based in the motherland, even if such an interpretation simply exchanged the objects to which positive and negative connotations were ascribed. As a result, Partisans have simply been transformed into criminals and bandits, while "national traitors" – as they used to be called in previous times – have become fighters for freedom and Western democracy as well as coming to be viewed as legitimate representatives of the Slovenian nation in relation to the Yugoslav government in exile and the international Allied community. The view according to which Partisans' opponents are regarded as benign and kindhearted pro-Western and pro-democratic enthusiasts who entirely meet today's (European) standards has won considerable recognition. According to this interpretation, what we are seeing today could be referred to as the triumph of the defeated.[48] Such a view is consistently embraced in the works of the historian Tamara Griesser Pečar, in particular in her monograph *Das zerrissene Volk*, published by the eminent publishing house Böhlau Verlag.[49] In 2005, it received the prestigious Anton Gindely Prize from the Institute for the Danube Region and Central Europe in Vienna. The late German legal expert Dieter Blumenwitz sought to provide legal arguments for Griesser Pečar's hypotheses in his legal study *Okkupation und Revolution in Slowenien (1941–1946): Eine völkerrechtliche Untersuchung*.[50] Blumenwitz is also the author of a legal opinion letter in which he opposed the standpoints of Jochen Frowein, who had prepared a legal study for the European Parliament in which he argued that from the legal point of view, the Beneš decrees could not be regarded as obstacles to the accession of the Czech Republic to the European Union.

The treatment of war-related issues that – from an interpretive point of view – introduce no new findings into the Slovenian historiography and Slovenian society as a whole, could hardly be defined as revision. Such efforts are, in fact, the very opposite of what revision should yield: new attempts to address and question the wartime past. In the afore-mentioned example of how old myths were undone in order to introduce new ones, one can observe merely schematic, ideological and biased attempts to rehabilitate the defeated Slovenian forces who had been tarnished by collaboration.[51]

---

48 Branko Rozman (ed.), *Slovenija 1941–1945. Zmagoslavje premaganih* (Ljubljana: Družina, 1995).
49 Tamara Griesser-Pečar, *Das zerrissene Volk. Slowenien 1941–1946. Okkupation, Kollaboration, Bürgerkrieg, Revolution* (Vienna–Cologne–Graz: Böhlau Verlag, 2003). Slovenian translation: *Razdvojeni narod. Slovenija 1941–1945. Okupacija, kolaboracija, državljanska vojna, revolucija* (Ljubljana: Mladinska knjiga, 2004).
50 Dieter Blumenwitz, *Okkupation und Revolution in Slowenien (1941–1946): eine völkerrechtliche Untersuchung* (Vienna–Cologne–Graz: Böhlau Verlag, 2005). Slovenian translation: *Okupacija in revolucija v Sloveniji (1941–1946): Mednarodnopravna študija* (Klagenfurt: Mohorjeva založba, 2005).
51 Bojan Godeša, "Spremembe v vrednotenju druge svetovne vojne na Slovenskem po padcu

Bearing the burden of collaboration, the opponents of the resistance movement (many of them emigrants) currently regard themselves as opponents of all forms of totalitarianism, and consistently present themselves as legal wartime representatives of the Slovenian population, who fought under the auspices of the Yugoslav government in exile against the Axis powers, thus siding with the antifascist coalition. Such an explanation has been dismissed in contemporary studies as an inaccurate interpretation of war events on Slovenian territory. Contrary to such an explanation, analyses have revealed an entirely different image of the anti-communist camp's engagement not only during the occupation, but also between the two World Wars. When Yugoslavia was attacked by the Axis powers in April 1941, the majority of the pre-war Slovenian political elite decided to tie their further existence to the destiny of the Axi A comprehensive survey of all the dimensions of such a policy among most of the pre-war political elite can be found in my book *Čas odločitev (Katoliški tabor in začetek okupacije)*, published by Mladinska knjiga in Ljubljana in 2011s powers, whose aim was to create a new totalitarian and racist order by waging war against the Allies. Their decision was based on their conviction that Hitler would win the war, with ideological motives (i.e. their affinity for fascism) present in the background, even if the majority of the Catholic camp had no serious scruples about adapting to the existing social order of the totalitarian states of Nazi Germany and Fascist Italy provided that the influence of the Catholic Church remained intact.[52]

The 1990s Demand for Reopening the Case Against the Ljubljana Bishop Dr. Gregorij Rožman

The perhaps most typical example of such an attempt was the reopening of the case against Dr. Gregorij Rožman, the Ljubljana bishop who was summoned to the Ljubljana Military Court in 1946. He was sentenced in absentia to "deprivation of liberty for a period of 18 years, to forfeiture of political and civil rights for a period of ten years after he has served the sentence, and to confiscation of all his property."[53] On 31 December 2005, the ordinary of the Ljubljana Archdiocese challenged the legality of the case, and on 1 October 2007, the Ljubljana Supreme

---

berlinskega zidu," in *Historični seminar 13*, edited by Katarina Šter and Mojca Žagar Karer (Ljubljana: Založba ZRC, 2018), 29–44.
52 A comprehensive survey of all the dimensions of such a policy among most of the pre-war political elite can be found in my book *Čas odločitev (Katoliški tabor in začetek okupacije)*, published by Mladinska knjiga in Ljubljana in 2011.
53 Marija Čipić Rehar, France Martin Dolinar, Tamara Griesser-Pečar, Blaž Otrin, and Julijana Visočnik, *Med sodbo sodišča in sodbo vesti. Dokumenti sodnega procesa proti škofu Gregoriju Rožmanu* (Ljubljana: Družina, 2009), 339.

Court annulled the decision of the Military Court of 29 August 1946. On 10 April 2009, the Ljubljana District Court stopped criminal proceedings against Bishop Rožman.[54] In 2013, Rožman's remains were exhumed and repatriated from the United States of America to Ljubljana Cathedral.

As early as in the 1980s, the Slovenian Catholic Church promoted a new evaluation of the engagement of the Church and Bishop Rožman during the occupation, an evaluation that was based on a scholarly confrontation with the "regime" thesis. The Church's stance was entirely clear at that time already: Rožman's cooperation with the occupiers could be explained exclusively as a result of his concern for the destiny of the Slovenian nation.[55]

Rožman's rehabilitation had been a primary goal of the Catholic Church in Slovenia all along. The Church wanted to have his case reopened to attain not only the legal annulment of the 1946 verdict, but above all to ensure the political and historical rehabilitation of his wartime deeds. Janko Pleterski commented on the Church's endeavours with the following words: "By no means will they leave the man[56] in history; they will strike while the iron is hot and turn him into a weapon for their current political agenda, they will objectify him in order to gain a kind of battering ram."[57] The official endeavours for the exhumation of Rožman's mortal remains and reburial in his motherland began in 1995, with the prerequisite for the bishop's reburial being his rehabilitation: "The unjust trial against Rožman has to be annulled first – otherwise Bishop Rožman should remain buried at the Franciscan cemetery in Lemont [Illinois]."[58] In the context of the imposition of such conditions, the Cardinal Secretary of State Angelo Sodano explained the Vatican's position in written correspondence with the then Slovenian President Kučan. According to the Holy See, "the reburial should depend on Rožman's legal and political rehabilitation."[59] Naturally, such endeavours implied not only a re-evaluation of Rožman's wartime role but also, in view of the symbolic significance and his vital role in the time of occupation, the rehabilitation of everything he stood for during the war. One of the key arguments for the proposal for reopening his case was alleged "new evidence," which supposedly exonerated him. Some of the evidence in fact already existed during the initial trial, but the Military Court refused to take this evidence into account

---

54 Ibid., 13–14.
55 ARS, Archives of the Republic of Slovenia: ARS 1931, Republic Secretariat for Internal Affairs, Box 3085, 'Nacionalno pomirenje' kao deo taktike unutrašnjeg i spoljnjeg neprijatelja (analitički osvrt) Belgrade, 4 March 1986.
56 i.e. Bishop Rožman.
57 Janko Pleterski, "Uvodna beseda," in Škof Rožman v zgodovini, edited by Janez Stanovnik, Slavko Grčar and Hardvik Pirnovar (Ljubljana: Društvo piscev zgodovine NOB Slovenije, 2008), 6.
58 Repe, Milan Kučan, 431–432.
59 Ibid.

even if it were familiar with it. However, it is also true that new incriminating evidence later came to light. Interestingly, this evidence was not taken into consideration or accurately contextualized in either of the works of two authors who offered historical expert opinion. This expert opinion was composed of two independent parts,[60] and served as the historical basis for the proposal to reopen the case. It is a fact that if the Military Court had had this evidence – especially a number of published diplomatic and military documents originating in Germany, Italy and the Vatican – at its disposal at the time of the trial, it would have found it much easier to pass a more transparent verdict, against which it would have been impossible to object from the point of view not only of historical credibility, but also legal order and the values of contemporary Slovenian society.[61] Even though the results of this investigation had not yet been presented at the time, President Kučan's opinion was that the reburial should not be contingent upon Bishop Rožman's legal and political rehabilitation, but should be regarded solely as a pious act, stemming from his right to a grave.[62] This was an opinion that Kučan expressed in his correspondence with the Cardinal Secretary of State Angelo Sodano. This opinion proved to be much more apposite, even from the point of view of historical credibility when the most recent historiographical findings were taken into consideration.

According to these findings, there are no verifiable reasons for Rožman's political rehabilitation. His political engagement was entirely in harmony with that of the political elite, which upon the Axis powers' attack on Yugoslavia tied its destiny to the former's success in the armed conflict with the Allies. As mentioned, this decision was based on the assumption that Hitler's victory was only a matter of time. Last but not least, it must be pointed out that in the autumn of 1941 Fascist Italy awarded Bishop Rožman an important state decoration for his engagement.[63]

The 2007 judgement of the Ljubljana Supreme Court, which annulled the 1946 verdict of the Military Court, can be better understood if one takes into account the 2009 decree of the Ljubljana District Court, which stopped the proceedings against the bishop. This decree was issued as a result of legal and procedural infringements: "[…] there were some infringements of the procedure from the

---

60 France Martin Dolinar and Tamara Griesser-Pečar, *Rožmanov proces* (Ljubljana: Družina, 1996).
61 Bojan Godeša, "O političnem delovanju ljubljanskega škofa dr. Gregorija Rožmana v prvih mesecih okupacije," *Zgodovinski časopis*, 67 (2013) 1–2: 152–170; Bojan Godeša, "O škofovi odgovornosti," *Mladina* (31 July 2015): 29; Bojan Godeša, "Enega mita ni mogoče zamenjati z drugim" (interviewed by Ženja Leiler), *Delo* (27 May 2016): 21.
62 Repe, *Kučan*, 431–432.
63 Godeša, "O političnem delovanju ljubljanskega škofa," 152–170; Godeša, "O škofovi odgovornosti."

point of view of putting on and conducting the said trial," and, given the absence of the defendant, "not all legally stipulated conditions were met."[64]

Conclusion

The introduction of interpretive pluralism in the second half of the 1980s and the subsequent changes that culminated in the accession of the Republic of Slovenia to the European Union in 2004 invite new reflections on the 1941–45 period in Slovenian historiography. As a result of new historiographical questions, the image of the wartime past has changed, the details have been enhanced, and the explanation of World War II that was prevalent in Slovenia before 1990 is no longer dominant in Slovenian historiography. In addition to numerous studies shedding light on wartime developments from different points of view, Slovenia has seen the publication of several comprehensive works addressing World War II in a balanced and multifaceted manner, seeking a historical synthesis.[65] Such works include: the papers published in the publication *Slovenska novejša zgodovina* ("Slovenian Recent History"),[66] the monograph *S puško in knjigo* ("With Guns and Books") by Božo Repe,[67] the monograph *Slovenija v vojni 1941–1945* ("Slovenia in the 1941–1945 War") by Zdenko Čepič, Damjan Guštin and Nevenka Troha,[68] as well as the compiled survey of the war published as a special issue of the magazine *Mladina*,[69] modelled upon similar editions of *Spiegel*, *Profil* and other magazines.

The basic characteristic of attempts to clarify the Slovenian wartime past consists of reconciliation efforts. If we tried to synthesize them, we might con-

---

64 Otrin, *Med sodbo sodišča in sodbo vesti*, 635–643.
65 The latest English-language survey of studies on World War II on Slovenian territory can be found in the study by Nevenka Troha, "Slovenia. Occupation, Repression, Partisan Movement, Collaboration, and Civil War in Historical Research. The Second World War in Historiography and Public Debate," *Südost-europa. Journal of Politics and Society* 65 (2017) 2: 334–363.
66 A collective two-column monograph written by historians from the Ljubljana Institute of Contemporary History: Zdenko Čepič, Neven Borak, Jasna Fischer, Bojan Godeša, Jurij Perovšek, Žarko Lazarević et al., *Slovenska novejša zgodovina. Od programa Zedinjene Slovenije do mednarodnega priznanja Republike Slovenije (1848–1992)* (Ljubljana: Mladinska knjiga, 2005).
67 Božo Repe, *S puško in knjigo. Narodnoosvobodilni boj slovenskega naroda 1941–1945* (Ljubljana: Cankarjeva založba, 2015).
68 Zdenko Čepič, Damijan Guštin, and Nevenka Troha, *Slovenija v vojni 1941–1945* (Ljubljana: Modrijan, 2017). The monograph is an updated version of *La Slovenia durante la seconda guerra mondiale* (Udine: Istituto friulano per la storia del movimento di liberazione di Udine, 2012), which was expanded and adapted for the Slovenian market.
69 Aleš Gabrič, Bojan Godeša, and Božo Repe, "Vojna v Sloveniji. Druga svetovna vojna (drugi del)," *Mladina (Posebna številka. Prispevki k razumevanju časa)* (3 December 2015).

clude by arguing that each declaration of reconciliation has only deepened antagonisms and ideological divisions in Slovenian society. It is obvious that the reconciliation concept/model has proved to be an exhausted and inadequate approach to solving problems in Slovenian society. Not only has it failed to solve existing problems, it has also created new ones.

Caught in the grip of the reconciliation process, Slovenian historiography has not yet managed to provide comprehensive answers to the basic dilemmas of World War II on Slovenian territory. The final unambiguous image of the war period has still to be shaped.

The saying "no truth, no reconciliation," which is nothing but a euphemism for rehabilitation (one which contemporary research has shown to be unjustified) of the side tarnished with war collaboration, has offered far too many opportunities for the politicization, manipulation and instrumental use of historiography. Such efforts have a considerable impact on the young generation (and, naturally, on society as a whole). This generation is still growing up in a biased and intolerant atmosphere that neither fosters understanding of nor sensitivity toward the past nor points out its contradictory and complex natures. Last but not least, such a situation has tarnished the social reputation of historiography, having undermined the credibility of the profession.

Marko Zajc

The Politics of Memory in Slovenia and the Erection of the Monument to the Victims of All Wars

This contribution aims to contextualize the erection of the Monument to the Victims of All Wars in Ljubljana (2017) as a complex phenomenon involving the official politics of memory of the Slovenian state, revisionist aspirations, and the ambivalence of the Slovenian public sphere regarding the traumatic past. Why are the concepts of national disunity and national reconciliation so prominent in Slovenian politics? Why was the monument erected and why is "no one pleased with it," as journalists cynically commented after its erection?

The concept of Slovenian national disunity first appeared in the Slovenian press in the nineteenth century, although the concept predominantly used at the time was that of "national unity."[1] Following the attack by Nazi Germany on Yugoslavia in April 1941, Slovenian territory was partitioned between Germany, Italy, Hungary, and the Independent State of Croatia.[2] The Slovenian communists, along with left-liberal and Christian Socialist groups, established the Liberation Front, which engaged in armed resistance against the Axis forces. The Slovenian Partisans were clearly successful: they emerged victorious from the war and, largely unassisted, liberated Slovenian territory. They also made successful steps toward establishing Slovenia as a political entity (for the first time in history) with new western borders, forming part of a new federal Yugoslavia. In doing so, the Partisans attained – at least to some degree – the old political dream pursued by the Slovenian national movement of 1848: a United Slovenia.[3]

There is a dark side to the Slovenian Partisan movement as well, one that is inextricably linked to the concepts of disunity and reconciliation. While the

---

1 Peter Vodopivec, *Od Pohlinove slovnice do samostojne države. Slovenska zgodovina od konca 18. do konca 20. stoletja* (Ljubljana: Modrijan, 2006), 87.
2 Zdenko Čepič, Damijan Guštin, and Nevenka Troha, *Slovenija v vojni 1941–1945* (Ljubljana: Modrijan, 2017), 43.
3 Božo Repe, *S puško in knjigo. Narodnoosvobodilni boj slovenskega naroda* (Ljubljana: Cankarjeva založba, 2015), 168–234; Joachim Hösler, "Sloweniens historische Bürde, Bundeszentrale für politische Bildung," available at: http://www.bpb.de/apuz/29421/sloweniens-historische-buerde?p=all (accessed 3 April 2018).

Partisan units were struggling against the Axis forces, conservative political forces, driven by their fear of communism, organized an anti-Communist militia under the auspices of the Italian authorities. An important role was played by the clergy and members of rightist Catholic organizations,[4] who, following the capitulation of Fascist Italy in 1943, organized the Slovenian Home Guard movement under the aegis of the German Army. The Home Guard participated in carrying out the German authorities' repressive measures (executions, deportations to concentration camps, and torture).[5] The new Slovenian communist leaders, viewing themselves as the vanguard of not only the proletariat, but also of the Slovenian "nation of proletarians," sought to maintain their power by any means possible. Immediately after the war, the new government summarily killed over eleven thousand Home Guard troops that had been repatriated by the British Army in Carinthia,[6] and executed members of various quisling formations from other parts of Yugoslavia, notably Croatia, who were captured in Slovenian territory at the end of the war.

From 1997 to 2012, researchers based at the Institute of Contemporary History in Ljubljana undertook systematic research into the victims of World War II and the post-war violence in the territory of what is present-day Slovenia. A total of 99,931 people, representing over 6.7 % of the population at that time, died as a result of the war. Partisan units suffered 28,444 casualties and counter-revolutionary units 15,514, most of whom died in the mass killings committed immediately after the war.[7] Other human losses were recorded among the civilian population. The research conducted by the Institute of Contemporary History identified about 15,000 victims of the post-war reckoning (including the civilian and non-civilian population, post-war killings, trials, camps, missing persons, and repression). Post-war killings claimed the lives of 11,616 Home Guard troops and 1,403 civilians.[8] It should be borne in mind that the research did not include victims with their permanent residence registered outside of the territory of what is presently Slovenia.

---

4 Čepič at al., *Slovenija v vojni*, 234–238.
5 Čepič et al., *Slovenija v vojni*, 317; Boris Mlakar, "Vseslovenska protirevolucionarna akcija," in Jasna Fischer (ed.), *Slovenska novejša zgodovina 1848–1992* (Ljubljana: Mladinska knjiga, 2005), 702.
6 Vida Deželak Barič, "Posledice vojnega nasilja: Smrtne žrtve druge svetovne vojne in zaradi nje na Slovenskem," in *Nasilje vojnih in povojnih dni*, edited by Nevenka Troha (Ljubljana: Inštitut za novejšo zgodovino, 2014), 34, 35.
7 Čepič et al., *Slovenija v vojni*, 429.
8 Deželak Barič, "Posledice vojnega nasilja", 36.

Concepts

When talking about how a society remembers past traumatic events and processes, such as World War II and the post-war killings, the question is not only that of what is being discussed, but also of what discourse or set of concepts are being used.[9] Even a quick glance at the literature on remembering and forgetting is enough to reveal the conceptual diversity. The concept most often used in reference to such traumatic episodes in the past is "transitional justice"[10] – a concept found in legal and political science literature on the topic, as well as in publications by non-governmental organizations.[11] The volume of literature on transitional justice is enormous, spanning historical comparisons, analyses of individual cases,[12] and handbooks on how transitional justice can be put to concrete use in divided societies. According to the International Center for Transitional Justice, the principle mechanisms through which it can be achieved are criminal prosecutions, truth commissions, reparation programmes, endeavours to achieve gender equality, security system reforms, and, finally, memorialization efforts.[13]

Transitional justice is closely associated with the concept of reconciliation. In post-conflict studies, reconciliation primarily stands for the way in which a society approaches life after a violent conflict, in enabling former enemies to live side by side.[14] Such a broad conceptualization of reconciliation correlates closely with the concept of transitional justice, because it encompasses the desire for both peace and justice. There is a consensus in conflict studies regarding which elements a reconciliation process should contain: revealing the truth about what happened, the perpetrators' acknowledgment of the harm done, contrition expressed through apology, forgiveness, exercising a right in some form, preventing the repetition of atrocities in the future, further pursuit of the con-

---

9 Reinhart Koselleck, *Vergangene Zukunft. Zur Semantik geschichtlicher Zeiten* (Frankfurt am Main: Suhrkamp, 1995), 107–130.
10 Jon Elster, *Closing the Books. Transitional Justice in Historical Perspective* (Cambridge: Cambridge University Press, 2004), 77.
11 Olivera Simić and Zala Volčič (eds.), *Transitional Justice and Civil Society in the Balkans* (New York: Springer, 2013), 1.
12 Jovana Mihajlović Trbovc and Vladimir Petrović, "The Impact of the ICTY on Democratization in the Yugoslav Successor States," in *Building Democracy in the Yugoslav Successor States. Accomplishments, Setbacks, Challenges since 1990*, edited by Sabrina Ramet (Cambridge: Cambridge University Press, 2017), 135–162.
13 International Center for Transitional Justice, https://www.ictj.org/about (accessed 4 April 2018).
14 Yaacov Bar-Siman-Tov, "Why Reconciliation?" in *From Conflict Resolution to Reconciliation*, edited by Yaacov Bar-Siman-Tov (Oxford: Oxford University Press, 2004), 3.

structive aspects of relations, and gradual restoration of trust.¹⁵ According to the ICTJ, a reconciliation process can only be sustained if those who committed violent crimes acknowledge their guilt in a way that is meaningful for the victims. Conversely, a reconciliation process should not impose the burden of forgiveness on the victims without demanding accountability from the perpetrators.¹⁶

The literature on transitional justice and reconciliation assigns major importance to the past and to the reconstruction of memory. Because dealing with the past has a therapeutic effect, the use of psychological and medical terms such as healing, therapy, and health is common.¹⁷ This is understandable to some degree, considering that conflict studies point to the psychological harm violence inflicts on individuals, while also employing psychological and medical analogies in reference to post-conflict societies. Although history is often mentioned, the focus is not on a historiographical analysis of conflicts.

In addition to the multi-branched paradigm of transitional justice, which moves somewhere between academic theory and "practical" conflict-solving, there is yet another international humanities tradition of studying traumatic events in the past. However, rather than concentrating on traumatic episodes in the past, this vast tradition of historiography and cultural studies focuses on remembering and historicizing events and processes.¹⁸ It deals not only with victims, but with the entire historical and social context. This tradition, too, uses the concept of memory, yet in a different way. Memory is essentially an individual phenomenon: two people can never share the same memories. However, individual memory cannot exist outside of society, because it is determined by it. The concept of collective memory is widely used in memory studies, albeit often critically.¹⁹ The distinction that some authors make between collective memory and "collected" memory corresponds to such a distinction between the individual and collectivist perception of the phenomenon of memory.²⁰

Another crucial concept is that of historical revisionism.²¹ Particularly of

---

15 Joanna Santa-Barbara, "Reconciliation," in *Handbook of Peace and Conflict Studies*, edited by Charles Webel and Johan Galtung (London, New York: Routledge, 2007), 176.
16 International Center for Transitional Justice, "Reconciliation," available at: https://www.ictj.org/gallery-items/reconciliation (accessed 3 April 2018).
17 Santa-Barbara, "Reconciliation," 176.
18 Florence Vatan and Marc Silberman, "Introduction. After the Violence: Memory," in *Memory and Postwar Memorials. Confronting the Violence of the Past*, edited by Florence Vatan and Marc Silberman (New York: Palgrave Macmillan, 2013), 1.
19 Wulf Kansteiner, "Finding Meaning in Memory. A Methodological Critique of Collective Memory Studies," *History and Theory* 41 (2002) 2: 179–197.
20 Jeffrey K. Olick, "Collective Memory. The Two Cultures," *Sociological Theory* 17 (1999) 3: 333–348.
21 Aviezer Tucker, "Historiographic Revision and Revisionism: The Evidential Difference," in *Past in the Making. Historical Revisionism in Central Europe after 1989*, edited by Michal Kopeček (Budapest, New York: CEU Press, 2008), 1–16.

interest for the subject at hand is the presence of historical revisionism in post-communist countries, where attempts to achieve national reconciliation have been tied to the radical reinterpretation of the past, with the intention of reinforcing a national agenda. A revisionist reading of the past represents not only the struggle for the interpretation of past events and structures, but also part of a search for the ideal "we" in the present. Rather than the past itself, debates on "historical truths" reveal more about the fragility and plurality of identities and policies aiming to strengthen the definition of national identity. From the vantage point of methodology, historical revisionism builds on a "descriptive self-sufficient manner of interpretation," the main characteristics of which are: a focus on the national framework, disregard for chronology, and/or de-historicization of the past, and moralization.[22]

To summarize: there are very few points of contact between the two traditions of interpreting violent events/processes in the past as presented above (transitional justice/conflict studies and historical revisionism studies/memory studies). Obviously, they convey very different perspectives – works on transitional justice do not use the concept of historical revisionism, but rather focus on "uncovering the truth" and on having a therapeutic impact on society. The most pronounced difference between the two lies in their respective attitudes toward the concept of reconciliation. Whereas the literature on transitional justice regards it as an ideal state, memory and revisionism studies treat it with scathing criticism.

The discrepancy between the literature on transitional justice and memory studies provides ample opportunities for proponents of historical revisionism. In Slovenia, the discourse of transitional justice was espoused by the advocates of historical revisionism, along with psychological and medical analogies used at both individual and national levels.[23]

From an obelisk to a monument

The first to speak in public in Slovenia about the killings of Home Guard troops was one of the Partisan leaders, Christian Socialist, and the poet Edvard Kocbek in 1975. However, the traumatic episodes of the wartime and post-war periods were not fully addressed until after Tito's death in 1980.[24] The question of the

---

22 Oto Luthar, "Red Dragon and the Evil Spirits," in *Of Red Dragons and Evil Spirits. Post-Communist Historiography between Democratization and New Politics of History*, edited by Oto Luthar (Budapest: CEU Press, 2017), 8–9.
23 Jože Dežman, "Preseganje travmatskih bremen titoizma," *Bogoslovni vestnik* 74 (2014) 4: 611–638.
24 Božo Repe, "Povojna represija v nacionalni identiteti in kolektivnem spominu Slovencev," in

Monument to the Victims of All Wars was raised at the very beginning of the public debate on the post-war killings, in 1984. In her essay "Krivda in greh" ("Guilt and Sin," from a collection of papers on Kocbek), the sociologist and unconventional intellectual Spomenka Hribar maintained that the Home Guard troops had also fought for their homeland, and emphasized that Slovenians would not attain true peace until both sides "in the civil war" admitted their guilt and sin. The left (notably, the communists) should acknowledge the killings and the revolution, and the right its collaboration with fascism and associated crimes. Without reconciliation, it was only a matter of time until the latent civil war would break out once again into a full-blown conflict. This assertion – which sounded particularly blasphemous in the context of that time, given that the socialist Slovenia was ideologically premised on the "national liberation struggle" – was that the Home Guard troops who were killed were also part of the Slovenian nation. In making this connection, Hribar proposed erecting an obelisk "that would scream the tragedy of a small nation," bearing a simple inscription: "Died for the Homeland."[25] An image of the Slovenian nation as a subject that must confront its past as a kind of collective person fits the "descriptive self-sufficient manner of interpretation" (a focus on the nation, de-historicization, and moralism).[26] As Lev Centrih points out, this is in line with the rule that the nation and the homeland are understood as a priori given traits of every individual, set apart from political, ideological, and productive practices.[27]

In 1990, following the first multiparty election, a reconciliation ceremony took place at the mass graves in the forest at Kočevje Rog, where the President of Slovenia shook hands with the Archbishop of Ljubljana.[28] After independence, the discourse of national reconciliation was espoused by the Slovenian conservative right.[29] In her article "Ustavimo desnico" ("Stop the Right"), published on 18 April 1991, Spomenka Hribar warned of the right's inflammatory campaign which, among other things, had also had an adverse effect on the process of national reconciliation.[30] Following this, Hribar was denounced by the political right as a leftist. The revisionist right started to actively encroach on the memory

---

Žrtve vojne in revolucije, edited by Janvit Golob, Peter Vodopivec, Janko Prunk, Tine Hribar, and Milena Basta (Ljubljana: Državni svet Republike Slovenije, 2005), 52.
25 Spomenka Hribar, "Krivda in greh," in *Kocbekov Zbornik*, edited by Dimitrij Rupel (Maribor: Obzorja, 1990), 61.
26 Luthar. "Red Dragon and the Evil Spirits," 8–9.
27 Lev Centrih, "Polemike o Drugi svetovni vojni v Sloveniji," *Borec* 60 (2008) 648–651, 71.
28 Božo Repe, *Slovenci v osemdesetih letih* (Ljubljana: Zveza zgodovinskih društev Slovenije, 2001), 68.
29 Tone Drobnič, "Slovenska zaveza," *Zaveza*, 10 February 1991: 2.
30 Janja Slabe, "Slovenska narodna sprava v časopisju (1984–1997)" (thesis), University of Ljubljana, Faculty of Arts, 2004: 80–85.

landscape by colonizing the central areas of parish graveyards. Breda and Oto Luthar analyzed Home Guard monuments and identified some of their fundamental concepts: reconciliation premised on relativizing collaboration with fascism, and switching the roles of perpetrators and victims, reinterpretation of the resistance movement and collaboration by blending them into an overarching concept of fratricidal war, pathologizing the Partisan resistance, presenting communism as emphatically non-Slovenian, and seeking national consensus based on homogenization.[31]

Due to conflicting views of history, some journalists and public intellectuals frequently resort to framing the concept of national disunity in terms of a simplistic interpretation of complex political problems.[32] Although most media columnists and public intellectuals approach the concept of national disunity critically, in a sense they also construct it. Writers of various political beliefs regard this dichotomy as something typically Slovenian: when it comes to history, they view Slovenia as divided into two more or less equal blocs. Public opinion surveys, however, offer a different view: most Slovenian citizens regard the Slovenian Partisan movement as positive (73.8 % in 1995 and 72.5 % in 2012).[33]

In early March 2009, the Commission on Concealed Mass Graves in Slovenia discovered a mass grave in the abandoned mine at Huda Jama. Photographs of mummified bodies, the remnants of uniforms, and women's braids in a mineshaft sent shockwaves across the Slovenian public,[34] and mobilized the centre-left Borut Pahor government. On 8 September 2009, the National Assembly adopted a special Law on War Grave Sites, stipulating, among other things, that a Monument to the Victims of All Wars be erected in the national capital. What is interesting is that the National Assembly also determined the monument's inscription, which subsequently became a point of contention (to be later discussed).[35] The parliamentary right did not support the Law and the project for the Monument to the Victims of All Wars remained tied to the centre-left and

---

31 Breda Luthar and Oto Luthar, "Kolonizacija spomina, Politika in kontekstualnost domobranskih spomenikov po letu 1991," in *Zbornik Janka Pleterskega*, edited by Oto Luthar and Jurij Perovšek (Ljubljana: Založba ZRC, 2003), 660.
32 Blaž Petkovič and Jože Poglajen, "Razklana politika je tipična slovenska značilnost," *Dnevnik*, 26 November 2012, avaliable at: https://www.dnevnik.si/1042564933 (accessed March 28, 2018).
33 Maca Jogan, "Majavo poznavanje zgodovine ne pelje v varno prihodnost," *Delo*, 31 August 2013: 6.
34 Ana Svenšek, "Huda jama je bila prehuda, po državi še vedno stotine neoznačenih grobišč," *Prvi interaktivni multimedijski portal, MMC RTV Slovenija*, 3 March 2015, available at: https://www.rtvslo.si/slovenija/huda-jama-je-bila-prehuda-po-drzavi-se-vedno-stotine-neo znacenih-grobisc/359553 (accessed 28 March 2018).
35 "Zakon o spremembah in dopolnitvah Zakona o vojnih grobiščih (ZVG-A)," *Pravno-informacijski sistem Republike Slovenije*, available at: http://www.pisrs.si/Pis.web/pregled Predpisa?id=ZAKO5691# (accessed 28 March 2018).

liberal side of the political spectrum. As evident from the minutes of the assembly session, the discovery of the grave at Huda Jama had had an inflammatory effect on the debate.[36]

Besides the revisionist right, the story of Huda Jama had also engrossed the cultural sphere. The fate of Mehmedalija Alić, the head of excavations in the mine, was first published by the newspaper *Delo* in 2010. Originally from Srebrenica, Alić was an adolescent when he came to Slovenia, where he completed his education and found work in the mining industry. Following the disintegration of Yugoslavia, Alić was illegally erased from the register of permanent residents, along with thousands of other immigrants residing in Slovenia from elsewhere in the former Yugoslavia. Although he eventually obtained Slovenian citizenship, he also struggled with the loss of two brothers in the Srebrenica genocide. As the miner who had torn down the final barriers before reaching the mass grave at Huda Jama, Alić began to fight for the victims' right to a decent burial.[37] The story of "a man touched by three evils: Srebrenica, erasure from the register, and Huda Jama" inspired the movie *Rudar* (The Miner), directed by Hanna Slak, with its premiere in 2017.[38]

In early 2010, the Ministry of Labour, Family, Social Affairs, and Equal Opportunities set up a monument project group led by Spomenka Hribar. The group decided that the monument should occupy the north side of Congress Square in Ljubljana – a location that was not under initial consideration at that time. The architect and Ljubljana Deputy Mayor Janez Koželj, for instance, believed it more appropriate for the monument to be erected in Žale, the city's central cemetery. However, as the documentation reveals, visualizing its symbolism (the centre of Slovenia's capital, near the parliament and government buildings), Hribar zealously advocated for the monument to be erected in Congress Square, which ultimately happened.[39] The implementation of the public tender for selecting an architectural concept for the monument was entrusted to the Chamber of Architecture and Spatial Planning.[40] As the public

---

36 "Stenografski zapisniki 12. izredne seje Državnega zbora RS z dne 8. 9. 2009," *Državni zbor RS*, available at: https://www.dz-rs.si/wps/portal/Home/deloDZ/seje/evidenca?mandat=V &type=sz&uid=73B7CF38A0C52997C12579680059E79C (accessed 28 March 2018).
37 Boštjan Videmšek, "Usoda," *Delo*, 17 July 2010, available at: http://www.delo.si/novice/svet/usoda.html (accessed 29 March 2018).
38 Vesna Milek, "Res verjamem v to, da človek lahko reši drugega človeka," *Delo*, 30 September 2017, available at: http://www.delo.si/sobotna/res-verjamem-v-to-da-clovek-lahko-resi-drugega-cloveka.html (accessed 29 March 2018).
39 "Zapisnik 4. seje projektne skupine za izvedbo projektov postavitve spomenika in izgradnje centralne kostnice," *Ministry of Labor, Family, and Social Affairs*, 22 April 2010.
40 "Spomenik vsem žrtvam vojn," *Ministry of Labor, Family, Social Affairs, and Equal Opportunities*, available at: http://www.mddsz.gov.si/si/medijsko_srediсce/novica/8200 (accessed March 28, 2018).

tender expressly stated, the monument should commemorate "the great number of inhabitants of Slovenian territory who died as soldiers of various armies in all wars, especially in the First and Second World Wars. It [should] also be dedicated to the numerous civilian victims of war and the revolution."[41]

The winning project, designed by the architectural firm Medprostor, envisaged a monument in the form of two tall concrete monoliths of differing dimensions, but of identical height and weight. The architectural composition was intended to reflect "unity in duality, a dialogue between two equal but different pillars representing the foundation of reconciliation, and an opportunity to create a common history." National reconciliation was to be embodied in the structure itself: two pillars connected via the same foundation, and concrete containing gravel and stones from Slovenian rivers.[42] The essential conceptual premise of the monument is therefore to simultaneously demonstrate the division and unity of the Slovenian nation. The lines engraved on it were written by Oton Župančič (1878–1949), one of the most prominent Slovenian poets:

> One homeland is
> Given to all,
> And one life
> And one death.

If one disregards the fact that the lines present a nationalist perception of social reality (the rule that a person can only have one homeland), they make an ideal inscription: all that the Slovenes have in common is life, death, and their homeland. However, the above verse is hardly ideologically neutral. Župančič supported the Partisan struggle and wrote the poem for the Tomb of People's Heroes, which was built in 1949 beside what is now the parliament building. Designed by the architect Edo Mihevc and the sculptor Boris Kalin, it serves not only as a memorial, but also as a veritable tomb, where during that same year ten Partisan people's heroes were buried, including the legendary commander Franc Rozman (nom de guerre – Stane). In 1979, the last remains to be placed in the tomb were those of the chief architect of socialist Yugoslavia, Edvard Kardelj.[43] The tomb stands less than four hundred meters from the site of the Monument to the Victims of All Wars. What is of significance here, however, is that the old monument bears two additional stanzas of Župančič's poem:

> Committed to freedom,
> We've gathered to fight;
> And what is life

---

41 "Natečajna naloga," *Gradnja spomenika žrtvam vseh vojn*, available at: http://zrtvamvojn.si/index.php/home/razvojprojekta/natecajna-naloga (accessed 4 April 2018).
42 Ibid.
43 "Grobnica narodnih herojev," *Dogovori* (16 February 1979): 6.

And what is death?
The future is faith!
Who dies for it,
Rises to life
When falling to death.⁴⁴

Apart from the fact that the chosen verses are devoted to Partisan heroes, together with the other two stanzas, they express a completely different message: it is worth dying for a better future. In other words, those who perished in the fighting did not die in vain. This obvious attempt at reinterpreting a dedicated poem attains the desired effect by simply removing it from the wider context. The parliamentary minutes reveal that the inscription was decided upon by the parliamentary left, not the revisionist right. Who, then, truly brought about the reinterpretation of Župančič's verse? Judging by her article from 2015, it is safe to suggest that it was Spomenka Hribar. In that article, the philosopher explained that the question concerning the monument was first raised following the first multiparty election in 1990. She purportedly did not insist on the original inscription: "There is no substantive difference between Župančič's lines 'One homeland is / Given to all, / And one life / And one death' and 'Died for the Homeland'. Such an inscription was finally accepted and legally endorsed." Hribar stressed that the wording was met with opposition from the political right, "on the grounds that the same lines are already engraved on monuments to the revolution." She dismissed such reasoning as one-dimensional and unmannered, "because poetry rises above all boundaries of ideology and time." With this statement she achieved two things. First, she justified the reinterpretation/revision of the poem and its isolation from the contemporary context by referring to poetry's timelessness and transcendentality, and, second, she accused the revisionist right of rejecting the inscription, even though the inscription was criticized by all sides of the political spectrum, including the left.⁴⁵

In the same article, Hribar distanced herself from the winning project because its symbolism did not correspond to her version of reconciliation. The communist-led Partisan struggle had two dimensions: the revolution (the bad one), and the struggle against Nazism and fascism accompanied by national liberation (the good one). Therefore, complete revisionism could not be deemed acceptable. Hribar did not agree with the representation of the two-pillar disunity of Slovenians, and she maintained that the monument was dedicated to the victims

---

44 Ibid.
45 Spomenka Hribar, "Spomini, ki družijo, spomini, ki ločujejo," *Mladina*, 21 August 2015, available at: http://www.mladina.si/168812/spomini-ki-druzijo-spomini-ki-locujejo (accessed 30 March 2018).

of not only World War II, but of all wars, including the 1991 Slovenian Independence War. Moreover, the monument reflects the current disunity and transfers it to the victims.[46]

A media analysis of the inauguration ceremony: focal points and interpretation[47]

The Monument to the Victims of All Wars was inaugurated on 13 July 2017. Below, I analyze the media coverage the event received in the ensuing weeks, when debates over its legitimacy reached a fever pitch. From the project launch up until its inauguration, the monument found its most fervent supporter in the Slovenian President Borut Pahor, who held the office of prime minister when the Act was adopted in 2009. The former leader of the Slovenian Social Democratic Party won the 2012 presidential election as an independent candidate by also receiving votes from the right-oriented base.[48] During his presidential term, Pahor (his use of social media also earned him the nickname the "King of Instagram")[49] completely internalized the discourse of (moderate) national reconciliation along the lines of "reconciliation is not about changing the past but changing the future."[50]

The president was, as expected, the speaker of honour at the inauguration ceremony, which was also attended by the Archbishop of Ljubljana and the Metropolitan Stanislav Zore, who delivered a prayer for the victims. The president demonstrated his appreciation of the importance of the politics of memory. "What we are, we are because of our memories. That is not to say that they are identical, uniform, or even the same. They are, however, shared." On the one hand, Pahor tried to position himself as a cosmopolitan, tolerant of different perceptions of national history. Yet, on the other hand, his speech bore the basic traits of historical determinism, emphasizing national cohesion free from exclusivism. Pahor is "proud to be a Slovene"; however, not because of a sense of superiority, but because he has no sense of inferiority of any kind.[51]

---

46 Ibid.
47 I am thankful to Oto Luthar for this material (a media clipping).
48 Jure Trampuš, "Janševa zmaga," *Mladina*, 7 December 2012, available at: http://www.mladina.si/118472/janseva-zmaga/ (accessed 4 April 2018).
49 Vasja Jager, "Kralj instagrama," *Mladina*, 18 August 2017, available at: http://www.mladina.si/181458/kralj-instagrama/ (accessed 4 April 2018).
50 Borut Pahor, "Sprava ni spreminjanje preteklosti, je spreminjanje prihodnosti," available at: http://www.predsednik.si/up-rs/uprs.nsf/objave/AF64FC03F2037A49C1257EBD00658640?OpenDocument (accessed 3 April 2018).
51 Borut Pahor, "Govor predsednika Republike Slovenije Boruta Pahorja na slovesnosti ob odprtju spomenika vsem žrtvam vojn in z vojnami povezanim žrtvam," 13 July 2017, avai-

Most of the leftist and rightist parliamentary opposition was absent from the opening ceremony. The left-wing party *Levica* ("The Left") described the project as a memorial to historical revisionism and spiritual darkness. The monument, according to The Left, completely negates the status and role of the Partisan struggle against fascism. The leader of the Slovenian Democratic Party, Janez Janša – the most vocal advocate of historical revisionism in the Slovenian political arena – once tweeted that "the war was as much to blame for the communist carnage as a rifle is to blame for murder." His comment pointed to the original evil of communism, which merely took advantage of World War II to assert its totalitarian dominance.[52]

The monument was also met with opposition from the Union of the Associations for the Values of the National Liberation Movement of Slovenia, which saw it as a new monument to discord. Besides noting that Župančič's lines were isolated from their context, the Union also protested the attendance of the Archbishop of Ljubljana, whose presence was against the principle of the separation of church and state. Conversely, the leader of the Slovenian Catholic Church, Archbishop Zore, welcomed the monument as an "opportunity to express our memory of and respect for all victims of war and revolutionary violence."[53] He made no mention of counter-revolutionary violence. Members of the Commission on Concealed Mass Graves in Slovenia, who led the excavations at Huda Jama, had something to say as well. The commission's head, Jože Dežman, – a proponent of historical revisionism, with a central focus on transitional justice – expressed his support for the monument, but added that it was merely, "the top of a bottomless pyramid." The monument would not be complete until all the dead were buried. A more lenient opposition was presented by the person in charge of probing and excavating the concealed graves, Mitja Ferenc, who first wanted the issue of the gravesites to be settled, and emotions to cool down.[54] An opinion poll carried out by the newspaper *Delo*, just days after the opening ceremony, found that 40 % of respondents approved of the monument, one quarter had reservations, and slightly over one quarter disapproved. When asked whether the Slovenian nation had reached a point of reconciliation with respect to its recent history, as many as 78 % of respondents answered negatively.[55]

Television reports tried to retain a certain amount of distance from the new monument, while at the same time reproducing the established discourse on

---

lable at: http://www.up-rs.si/up-rs/uprs.nsf/objave/D2FB2A48C140B6F7C125815C005D947C?OpenDocument (accessed 4 April 2018).
52 Ranka Ivelja and Meta Roglič, "Spomenik sprave ali spomenik razdora," *Dnevnik* (12 July 2017): 1.
53 Ibid, 2.
54 Vanessa Čokl, "Ti in jaz, oče in sin, belo in črno," *Večer* (12 July 2017): 4.
55 Zoran Potič, "Podpora odkritju spomenika vsem žrtvam vojn," *Delo* (17 July 2017), 2.

Slovenian disunity, and the need for national reconciliation. A national television journalist, highlighting the urgency of reconciliation, asked her guests: "When will reconciliation be possible in Slovenia?" The politicians in the studio responded by making similar statements: the monument is a step in this direction, and more forgiveness and reverence is needed.[56] Interesting coverage was provided by the commercial television station Kanal A, which took a much more critical stance toward the concept of reconciliation. The Kanal A presenter accused Slovenian politicians of exploiting the issue of reconciliation to score political points. What are the opinions of young people, who have no need for reconciliation? A short survey carried out among them on the streets found them to be completely indifferent to the monument. Some had no knowledge whatsoever of it, and others merely heard that it was a kind of peace gesture between the Home Guard troops and the Partisans. The show continued by presenting a few victims of the wartime and post-war violence: an Auschwitz survivor; a woman whose father was shot by the Partisans after the war; and the widow of a man who died in the 1991 Independence War. The presenter concluded the talk on a moralistic and antipolitical note, stating that politics has been exploiting history for twenty-six years, even though, clearly, the Home Guard troops collaborated with the Axis forces and the communists were the perpetrators of the post-war killings.[57]

The new monument received the most extensive coverage in the right-wing press, notably the magazine of the Slovenian Democratic Party, *Demokracija*. According to the commentator Metod Berlec, the erection of the memorial was "an act promoting the left's feigned desire for reconciliation." In his opinion, the reconciliation ceremony at Kočevje Rog in 1990 was used by former communists as a political coverup to prevent the police from investigating war crimes, and these criminals' successors have been minimizing the tragedy of the bloody revolution ever since. Because they feel no remorse for the crimes of their "political fathers," the new monument is nothing more than an embodiment of the distorted truth. Berlec objects to the tomb of "the leading communist executioners" (the Tomb of the People's Heroes) being located in the direct vicinity of the new monument.[58] The commentary was rounded off with a discussion by a well-known Home Guard member and revisionist, Justin Stanovnik, who once again placed the blame for the "civil war" on the communists. His six-page deliberation contains not a single mention of fascist collaboration.[59] The re-

---

56 "Odkritje spomenika na Kongresnem trgu," *TV Slovenija 1, Odmevi* (10 p.m.), 13 July 2017 (clipping), available at: https://4d.rtvslo.si/arhiv/odmevi/174481986 (accessed 4 April 2018).
57 "Postavitev spomenika sprave," *Kanal A, Svet* (6 p.m.), 13 July 2017 (clipping).
58 Metod Berlec, "V senci spomenikov množičnih morilcev," *Demokracija* (20 July 2017): 3.
59 Justin Stanovnik, "Spomenik žrtvam vseh vojn," *Demokracija* (20 July 2017): 1–6.

visionist reaction is clear and calls for a complete eradication of the hated symbols.

Architects and art historians criticized the monument even before the inauguration ceremony took place. The art historian Beti Žerovc disapproved of the selected project, among other things, for its failure to convey the content prescribed in the public tender. Rather than the victims of all wars, the monument commemorates the current (divided) stance present toward World War II, and its highlighted vertical axes embody a "male principle," subsuming subjugation instead of commemoration. She was one of the rare experts to problematize the notion of reconciliation. Such a monument will not facilitate social cohesion, but instead draw violence from the fringes into the heart of society.[60] The symbol of division was also rejected by the architect Marko Apih, who maintained that – lacking in substance – the monument only allows for individual interpretation.[61] Further criticism was voiced by the architect Fedja Košir, who described the monument as a "minimalist mass without a name and meaning."[62] Oton Župančič's granddaughter Alenka Župančič spoke up as well, explaining that the poem was dedicated to Partisan heroes. Nevertheless, the poet's relatives chose not to demand a ban on its use. The unauthorized copying of Župančič's verse was likewise condemned by the president of the Slovenian Writers' Association PEN, Ivo Svetina, who labelled the reinterpretation as "photocopying a new Slovenian affliction."[63]

Even before the inauguration, the monument took on a life of its own, beyond moral and political debates over national reconciliation and division. Interestingly, its mere presence affected the neighbouring buildings. By bizarre coincidence, a night club called "Pr' Skelet" ("The Skeleton") stands right next to the monument. Due to unsavoury associations (given that the monument commemorates the dead), the bar owner was asked to take down the sign before the opening event.[64] To further add to the irony, there is also a café near the monument called "Zvezda" ("The Star"). Just days before the unveiling, the following tweet by journalist Martin Tomažin went viral: "After the inauguration, the righties will probably sit down for a cup of coffee at Pr' Skelet, and the lefties will head down to get some ice cream at Zvezda."[65]

---

60 Beti Žerovc, "Spomenik, ki bo zapičen v naše osrčje za vselej," *Delo*, 18 March 2017, available at: http://www.delo.si/sobotna/spomenik-ki-bo-zapicen-v-nase-osrcje-za-vselej.html (accessed 4 April 2018).
61 Marko Apih, "Pisma bralcev," *Sobotna priloga Dela*, (22 July 2017): 30.
62 Fedja Košir, "Pisma bralcev," *Sobotna priloga Dela* (22 July 2017): 31.
63 Gregor Butala and Maja Šučur, "Neavtorizirano kopiranje Župančičevih verzov," *Dnevnik*, (15 July 2017): 2.
64 "Jankoviću obljubil, da bo umaknil tablo z imenom lokala." *Dnevnik* (13 July 2017): 9.
65 "Izjave tedna," *Mladina*, 28 July 2017, available at: http://www.mladina.si/181081/izjave-tedna/ (accessed 3 April 2018).

Conclusion

From 1984 to the present day, Spomenka Hribar has been projected in the Slovenian public eye either as an undisputed moral authority, or as a trouble-making publicist. The Slovenes are unable to muster enough distance from their past to tackle national reconciliation as a historical phenomenon, as was made manifest by a group of critical intellectuals during the 1980s, who in their critique of Yugoslav communism discovered the concept of nation. Just like the Romantic nationalists during the first half of the nineteenth century, they too recognized national emancipation as a solution to many of the ailments of modern society. In their view, the dominance of class over national identity was an indirect cause of the nationalisms in Yugoslavia.[66] Given Slovenia's traumatic past, they put the concept of national reconciliation at the heart of their agenda. Within a small number of years, regime critics (including Spomenka Hribar) were ascribed the role of national leaders, and their critique became the ideological backbone of the new state.

After the dust surrounding the new monument had settled in the summer of 2017, commentators for the central Slovenian newspaper *Delo* drew two conclusions: that no one wants the monument and that it has no substance. According to Jožica Grgič, the monument "is neither beautiful nor ugly because it is – empty,"[67] to which her colleague Peter Kolšek added that "no one historically sane" will be pleased with it.[68] However, is emptiness truly the main characteristic of the monument? From the perspective of the politics (and culture) of memory, the monument may justly be ascribed two meanings. First, it clearly manifests the ideology of Slovenian national disunity or division via its split into two more or less equal parts. This component has drawn criticism from both experts (art historians, architects, and historians) and politicians of different beliefs, not to mention the conceptual author of the monument. Nevertheless, a quick foray into the critiques of division reveals that only a few actually problematized national division as such, but rather focused on how the monument reflects different interpretations of World War II. In other words, the monument was supposed to commemorate the victims of all wars rather than merely reflect the rift over World War II and the post-war killings. Ignoring the fact that the idea of division is in itself controversial, the critics of the monument mainly resort to reconstructing the ideology of division and devising new reinterpretations of it. From the perspective of national historiography and memory studies, however,

---

[66] Ivo Urbančič, "Jugoslovanska 'nacionalistična kriza' in Slovenci v perspektivi konca nacije," *Nova revija* 5 (1987) 57: 36.
[67] Jožica Grgič, "Zidova kot spomenik," *Delo* (15 July 2017): 1.
[68] Peter Kolšek, "Metafizika v avgustu," *Sobotna priloga Dela* (5 August 2017): 32.

such a dualistic historical perception poses a problem because it prevents a more complex and pluralist view of the past from being formulated in the public sphere.

The second ideological component of the monument is so obvious that the critics completely failed to notice it: Slovenian nationalism. The only link connecting the commemorated victims of war is Slovenian national identity, whereas no consideration is given to pre-national, local, territorial, hybrid, and "foreign" identifications. If one has a monument materializing a moderate ideology of national reconciliation, and if one accepts that the concept of national reconciliation is indispensably premised on an understanding of the nation as a predetermined characteristic of individuals, then this monument represents an explicit materialization of the nation. Can the Monument to the Victims of All Wars be defined as the sole monument to pure Slovenian identity? Although this is a rhetorical question, it is impossible to conceive of such a monument without Slovenian nationalism.

Maruša Pušnik

Media-Based Historical Revisionism and the Public's Memories of the Second World War

The following article analyses the making of history from the top-down, with a special focus on media representations of World War II, and from the bottom-up, in investigating how people managed the World War II period through their memories. Writing at the intersection between popular memories and media history management, the author examines the position the media occupy in memory battles over Slovenia's contemporary history. The article posits that World War II, which also once signified a common Yugoslav identity, has become a convenient site for memory battles. The dominant media produce revisionist narratives of World War II, and, in doing so, incite audiences to blur old memories, and form new ones. What such a politics of memory effectively achieve is to obscure the paradigm of liberators versus aggressors, so that it is suddenly no longer clear who the aggressor was and who the liberator was during the war. This may have major cultural and political implications for the Slovenian nation.

Introduction: the collision of historical narratives and memories

Because many different, even conflicting, historical narratives of the same past event may circulate in social space, it is the dominant discourse in society – usually formed via dominant political, media, educational, and scientific discourses – that ordinarily grants hegemony to one discourse, transforming it over time into official history. Such a collision of different historical narratives is currently also unfolding in Slovenia, with irreconcilable historical interpretations of past events competing for the hegemonic status of absolute truth about the World War II past. The disintegration of Yugoslavia and the fall of the communist regime led not only to the creation of the independent Republic of Slovenia, but also to reinterpretations of the shared Yugoslav past, and especially World War II and the Partisan struggle. These are now continually at odds with the Home Guard and counter-revolutionary interpretations of the past.¹ In other words, during the Yugoslav period, the Partisan movement was the hallmark of the common state and then, with Yugoslavia's disintegration, it suddenly became subjected to reinterpretations and strong currents of historical revisionism.²

This article therefore deals with reinterpretations of historical themes such as World War II, the Partisan movement, counter-revolutionary organizations, and the Home Guard movement as several of the most bitterly contested topics facing Slovenia today. The focus is not on changing monuments, museum representations, and textbooks, nor on the renaming of streets and squares as central "sites of memory."³ Rather, of interest is the "landscape of people's memory"⁴ – that is, how people's memories change in society – on the one hand, and how media representations of these historical themes change on the other.⁵ This study

---

1 Following Germany's attack on Yugoslavia on 6 April 1941, the Liberation Front of the Slovenian Nation was established no later than 27 April 1941 and raised armed Partisan resistance against the Axis powers. Alongside this initial function, the National Liberation Struggle also had a secondary role – the communist revolution. The Yugoslav Partisan Movement was led by Josip Broz Tito, who also became the leader of the Communist Party of Yugoslavia. Soon after the attack, a civil war broke out throughout Yugoslav territory between the Partisans and counter-revolutionary organizations, such as the Village Guard, the White Guard, the Blue Guard, and subsequently the Home Guard, which was officially established in September 1943. What all these groupings primarily shared in common was the struggle against communist revolution. After the war and triumph over Nazism, the members of the collaborationist forces fled the country, but were captured by the Allies and returned to Yugoslavia, where many of them died as a result of extrajudicial executions. This – alongside the failure of the communist leadership in postwar Yugoslavia to clearly address the subject of postwar killings – is the reason why the period after World War II remains an inflammatory topic in Slovenia. The dominant historical narrative in Yugoslavia was crowned by the victory of the Partisan Movement, and the memory of the postwar killings was suppressed.
2 As Dejan Jović and Darko Suvin demonstrate, it was the Partisan wartime politics that enabled the formation of Yugoslavia as a revolutionary political entity that emerged during the war and made a radical break from the old conditions in the prewar Royalist Yugoslavia. See, e. g., Dejan Jović, *Yugoslavia: A State That Withered Away* (West Lafayette: Purdue University Press, 2009), 54; Darko Suvin, *Samo jednom se ljubi: Radiografija SFR Jugoslavije* (Belgrade: Rosa Luxemburg Stiftung, 2014), 314–318.
3 Pierre Nora, "Between Memory and History: Les Lieux de Mémoire," *Representations* 26 (special issue: *Memory and Counter-Memory*) (1989): 7–24.
4 Simon Schama, *Landscape and Memory* (New York: Alfred A. Knopf, 1995).
5 Historical revisionism of World War II has been at the focus of a number of Slovenian studies; see, e. g., Oto Luthar, Oto, "Preimenovanje in izključevanje kot sestavni del postkomunistične kulture spomina v Sloveniji," *Prispevki za novejšo zgodovino* 54 (2014) 2: 195–211; Oto Luthar, "Post-Socialist Historiography between Democratization and New Exclusivist Politics of History," in *Of Red Dragons and Evil Spirits: Post-Communist Historiography between Democratization and New Politics of History*, edited by Oto Luthar (Budapest: CEU Press, 2017), 187–207; Oto Luthar, "Post-Communist Memory Culture and the Historiography of World War II and the Post-War Execution of Slovenian Collaborationists," *Politička misao* 55 (2018) 2: 33–49; Maca Jogan and Živa Broder, "Samostojna Slovenija in kolektivni zgodovinski spomin," *Teorija in praksa* 53 (special issue, September 2016): 90–111; Irena Šumi, "Slovenski

therefore observes the ways in which bottom-up memories, or so-called popular memories,[6] meet, are impregnated by, and confront more authoritarian, top-down, and often already institutionalized memories.

The central research question is that of the role the media in Slovenia play in these cultural struggles to define the past or, rather, how media representations of World War II fuel memory battles in society by introducing revisionist narratives into public space. However, how people manage these representations, or how their memories of World War II are changing, is also of interest. The aim is to elucidate how the Partisan struggle and World War II, once deemed the connective tissue binding the Yugoslav republics together, became subject to reinterpretation in public space, and how they are now being used as signifiers of the undemocratic past. Studies of surging historical revisionism in the media are crucial for understanding how identities are being formed in the present, and how the past is (ab)used for the purposes of the present.

At present, there is no clear consensus regarding historical themes relating to World War II among the Slovenes, who are, in a way, divided into two sharply opposed camps: those who struggle for the revisionist writing of recent history, and those who struggle for the preservation and rejuvenation of revolutionary histories. Such struggles over historical interpretation are rampant across post-communist Eastern Europe, which has been witnessing attempts at reinterpreting the shared communist past, and often also the Partisan movement, as the foundation on which communist communities were created.[7] To para-

---

antisemitizem, živ pokopan v ideologiji slovenske narodne sprave," *Časopis za kritiko znanosti* 43 (2015) 260: 69–84; Maruša Pušnik, "Documentaries and Mediated Popular Histories: Shaping Memories and Images of Slovenia's Past," in *Technologies of Memory in the Arts*, edited by Liedeke Plate and Anneke Smelik (Basingstoke: Palgrave Macmillan, 2009), 188–202.

6 Michel Foucault, "Film and Popular Memory: An Interview with Michel Foucault," *Radical Philosophy* 11 (1975) 11: 24–29.

7 The sheer number of studies testifies to the currently exceptional level of interest across Eastern Europe in the reinterpretation of the communist and Partisan past. See, e. g., Cristian Tileagă, "Communism in Retrospect: The Rhetoric of Historical Representation and Writing the Collective Memory of the Recent Past," *Memory Studies* 5 (2012) 4: 462–478; Mitja Velikonja, "Lost in Transition: Nostalgia for Socialism in Post-Socialist Countries," *East European Politics and Societies* 23 (2009) 4: 535–551; Miklavž Komelj, "The Function of the Signifier 'Totalitarianism' in the Constitution of the 'East Art' Field," in *Retracing Images: Visual Culture after Yugoslavia*, edited by Daniel Šuber and Slobodan Karamanić (Leiden, Boston: Brill, 2012), 55–80; Tanja Petrović, "The Territory of the Former Yugoslavia in the 'Mental Maps' of Former Yugoslavs: Nostalgia for Space," *Sprawy Narodowościowe* 31 (2007): 263–273; Boris Buden, *Cona prehoda: o koncu postkomunizma* (Ljubljana: Založba Krtina, 2014); Ana Kladnik, "Conference Report: 'Socialism on the Bench'," *Social History* 41 (2016) 3: 319–325; Ulf Brunnbauer, *(Re)Writing History: Historiography in Southeast Europe after Socialism* (Münster: LIT Verlag, 2004); Maria Todorova, Augusta Dimou, and Stefan Troebst, *Remembering Communism: Private and Public Recollections of Lived Experience in Southeast Europe* (Budapest: CEU Press, 2014); Barbara Christophe, "An Analysis of Discursive Strategies in

phrase Todorova, one may see Slovenia as a space with similar trajectories, but different memories.[8] There is a collision of memories and – as is currently typical in Slovenia – this collision is also becoming increasingly institutionalized in museums, exhibitions, and textbooks, as well as in educational and public discourses.[9] Moreover, these debates are also politically instrumentalized and institutionalized,[10] with left-wing parties assuming a highly positive stance towards the Partisans' National Liberation Struggle, while right-wing parties extol the Home Guard Struggle, and treat the Partisan movement with contempt.[11]

This exploratory study therefore focuses on the power play between historical narratives and memories of World War II in Slovenian society. The analysis consists of two reflections. First, it analyses the role of various popular, or bottom-up, memories. Second, it examines top-down representations of World War II in the media. For this purpose, 174 semi-structured interviews with people born between 1923 and 1975 were completed to deconstruct and analyse various memories of World War II, as well as the Partisan and the Home Guard movements. However, in this research I only included those 116 interviews for which we have demographic data regarding the respondents. I divided the respondents into two groups: 58 interviews were conducted with the middle-aged (born between 1955 and 1975) generation, and 58 interviews with the older (born before 1955) generation in Slovenia. I formed two groups of respondents ac-

---

Lithuanian Textbooks," *Eckert. Beiträge* 10 (2010), http://repository.gei.de/bitstream/hand le/11428/89/644917660_2016_A.pdf?sequence =1&isAllowed=y; Emilia Palonen (25 August 2018), "The City-Text in Post-Communist Budapest: Street Names, Memorials, and the Politics of Commemoration," *GeoJournal* 73 (2008) 3: 219–230; Eva Kovács, "The Cynical and the Ironical: Remembering Communism in Hungary," *Transit 30 (2005/2006):* 155–169; Joseph Zajda and Rea Zajda, "The Politics of Rewriting History: New History Textbooks and Curriculum Materials in Russia," *International Review of Education* 49 (2003) 3: 363–384.

8 Maria Todorova, "Introduction: Similar Trajectories, Different Memories," in *Remembering Communism: Private and Public Recollections of Lived Experience in Southeast Europe,* edited by Maria Todorova, Augusta Dimou, and Stefan Troebst (Budapest: CEU Press, 2014), 1–26.

9 Wertsch writes about a similar chaotic situation concerning Second World War history instruction in Russian schools. See, e.g., James Wertsch, "The Narrative Organization of Collective Memory," *Ethos* 36 (2008) 1: 133, 120–135.

10 Farrel Corcoran, The Political Instrumentality of Cultural Memory: A Case Study of Ireland, in: *Javnost/The Public* 9/3 (2002), 49–63.

11 Similarly, according to Kosi (2012), it is characteristic of dominant ideologies in the post-communist transitional period in Slovenia that references to the history of World War II mark out a distinction between officially left-wing and right-wing parties. Buden (2014), however, finds the surge in revisionist discourses to be in line with nationalist projects in all post-Yugoslav societies. He defines them as the products of transitional ideologies insisting on a smooth transition to corporate capitalism. See, e.g., Jernej Kosi, "V vsaki situaciji se je treba boriti za pridobljene delavske pravice" (interview by Ana Svenšek), *MMC RTVSLO,* 11 November 2012, http://www.rtvslo.si/velikih-5/v-vsaki-situaciji-se-je-treba-boriti-za-pridobljene-delavske-pravice/295498 (1 September 2018); Buden. "Cona prehoda".

cording to their generational affiliation. I assumed that those born before 1955 as part of older generations have stronger direct or indirect experiences (through their parents' testimonies) of World War II and the post-war period, while those born in the middle generation had already gradually lost their stronger connection to the World War II period. Thus, this generation's memories are in a greater sense created through mediated testimonies and representations of World War II, compared to those of the older generation, whose memories are constructed to a greater degree through personal experiences or stronger familial ties and family members' testimonies. The interviews were conducted in 2015–2016 across the entire territory of Slovenia.[12]

Age		Gender		Residence		Educational level		
–1955	1955–75	Male	Female	Urban	Rural	Primary	Secondary	High
58	58	51	65	46	70	23	56	37

Table 1: Overview of age distribution, distribution by gender, residence and education.

Memory is treated in terms of the ideas and experiences presented by the respondents. In such a grass-roots (bottom-up) constitution of memory, Tileagă claims, "there are multiple perspectives and alternative ways of meaning-making that are sourced in the subjective standpoint of the social actor, experiences and 'typifications' of everyday life, and the seemingly anarchic interplay of 'well-informed' opinion in the public sphere."[13] The respondents are approached as "active agents," to borrow Wertsch's formulation, encompassing their own narratives and active micro-constructions of the past.[14] We asked respondents to formulate answers according to their own experiences of World War II and the post-war period (if they were old enough at that time), and according to their perceptions of recent explanations of World War II. The basic research questions guiding the interviews were as follows: What kinds of memories of World War II are formed when people become faced with these topics, either from their own experiences or from public discussions about such topics? How do respondents create their memories (through trauma, pleasant memories etc.)? How do they link the present with the past, and how does the past affect their present? These main research questions were also extremely helpful in investigating how their personal memories collide with mediated memories. The aim was to observe how the respondents constructed their memories from personal experiences on

---

12 The interviews are part of a wider project, conducted as part of the course Media and Collective Memory, where students investigated how memories of World War II, the Partisan Movement, Socialist Yugoslavia and communism have transformed in the late twentieth and twenty-first century in Slovenia. At this point, therefore, I would like to express my gratitude to the students.
13 Tileagă, "Communism in Retrospect," 464.
14 Wertsch, "The Narrative Organization of Collective Memory," 122.

the one hand, and from mediated remembering on the other. We mostly followed these points when both were mixed together.

On the other hand, this research also includes mediatized commemorative imagery of World War II, focusing mostly on the period after 2004 when revisionist discourses began to gain impetus in the media. Media reports on World War II, the National Liberation Struggle, and the Partisan movement published in the newspaper *Delo*[15] between 1 January 1989 and 1 August 2012 were examined. The analysis included 480 reports. *Delo* is one of the dominant media in Slovenia and is not a state-owned medium. However, it can be argued that the Slovenian state has had a significant impact on its reporting, and that this reporting is intertwined with the state's political discourses. In many cases there have been parallels between media and political discourses,[16] and *Delo* reports on the state political situation, often without critical reflection upon those political discourses, simply transmitting them. When in political discourse, the Home Guards vs. Partisans discourse comes to the fore, one can observe that this emphasis also occurs in *Delo's* discourse. Using this research model, a parallel study was undertaken of bottom-up and top-down narratives of the past, in order to demonstrate how popular memory is colliding with the mechanisms of Slovenian institutional media power. Although both empirical studies were carried out separately, I use them as parallel studies in this paper to show how popular memories of World War II align with media narratives of World War II. In other words, I interpret bottom-up memories through the prism of top-down media narratives and search for these nodal points, which are common or opposed in both empirical studies.

Top-down narratives: revisionist media discourses regarding World War II

The Slovenian media add a significant amount of fuel to the memory battles that are unfolding in public space, essentially and typically through their revisionist redefinition of the role of the anti-Fascist National Liberation Struggle and that of the collaborationist Home Guard.[17] Ever since the late 1980s, the media have

---

15 *Delo* was selected as one of the most widely read quality newspapers in Slovenia and as one of the oldest dailies in Slovenia; it started circulating as early as 1959, through the merger of two newspapers, Slovenski poročevalec, which was the official newspaper of the Liberation Front during World War II, and Ljudska pravica, the official newspaper of the Communist Party of Slovenia.
16 See also Mojca Pajnik, Medijsko-politični paralelizem: legitimizacija migracijske politike na primeru komentarja v časopisu "Delo", in: *Dve domovini/Two homelands* 45 (2017), 169–184.
17 Public opinion polls, too, point to the ongoing transformations of memories and popular

played a pivotal role in society with their gradual introduction of new narratives on World War II that challenged the previously dominant ones.[18] In the late 1980s and early 1990s, the themes of war and of post-war killings burst to the surface for the first time, and the media published an increasing number of reports on the subject. For example, between 1989 and 2000, *Delo* featured an unprecedented 192 reports (plus an additional 179 readers' letters) on the post-war killings (sixty-three in 1990 alone). This clearly confirms the thesis that revisionist interpretations started to make inroads into public space from the late 1980s onward.

As the analysis of the *Delo* material shows, a growing number of reports are concerned with "the disclosure of post-war slaughters"[19] or, even more illustratively, with the communist leaders who "have caused significant damage and more victims among the Slovenian nation than the two Axis forces, Nazism and Fascism, did together."[20] *Delo* started to treat the Partisan movement as completely equivalent to communism, and to demonize it by increasingly addressing the national reconciliation and rehabilitation of Home Guard troops as having been the Partisans' victims. The entire discussion concerning World War II became reduced to finding the perpetrators of the war and post-war killings, and all reports unanimously pointed in the direction of the Partisans. Some blamed the leadership of the Yugoslav Army,[21] others Josip Broz Tito,[22] and others the post-war Slovenian communist leaders,[23] who allegedly cooperated with the communist secret services.[24] Several even went as far as to place blame for the killings, which occurred half a century ago, on today's leftist political leaders

---

perceptions of World War II – perceptions of the Home Guard are becoming more positive with each year and, more alarmingly still, each year, people know less about the history of World War II. See, e.g., Niko Toš, "Vrednote v prehodu," in *Slovenija v evropskih primerjavah: evropska družboslovna raziskava 2002–2010*, edited by Niko Toš (Ljubljana: Fakulteta za družbene vede, 2012).

18 This coincides with the political event of the disintegration of Yugoslavia and the idea of national reconciliation, which had just started to surface, and the time when the public intellectual Spomenka Hribar wrote her philosophical essay "Krivda in greh" ("Guilt and Sin"), calling for a public and vocal discussion about the Partisans' wartime and postwar killings of the Home Guard troops.

19 Cvetko Zagorski, "Poglobimo delo komisij za odkrivanje povojnih morij," *Delo*, 14 March, 1991, p. 10.

20 Vinko Levstik, "O povojnih pobojih je odločalo vodstvo jugoslovanske armade," *Delo*, 18 July, 1992, p. 16.

21 Vinko Vasle, "O povojnih pobojih je odločalo vodstvo jugoslovanske armade," *Delo*, 1 July, 1992, p. 2.

22 Igor Guzelj, "Povojno 'čiščenje' je odobril Josip Broz," *Delo*, 1 December, 1993, p. 2.

23 Jože Biščak, "Slovenski vrh je vedel za poboje," *Delo*, 3 December, 1992, p. 3.

24 STA, "Imperij Matije Mačka je še vedno dejaven," *Delo*, 10 June, 1994, p. 2.

(pejoratively called the "forces of communist continuity").[25] According to this analysis, most newspaper articles highlighted the discursive framework characterized by equating the communist policy with the Partisan movement, as well as vilifying the anti-Fascist struggle and the Republic of Yugoslavia created during World War II. At the end of the 1980s, the media discourse introduced an entirely new vocabulary in relation to the Partisans and Yugoslavia, which, for the first time, also made its way into *Delo*. Furthermore, new labels were invented to convey meanings totally opposed to those previously used. These portrayed the Partisans, now equated with communists, as "slaughterers" perpetrating "massacres", turning the Home Guard troops into "victims." Such a vocabulary creates a melodramatic and spectacular moralizing frame for representing themes relating to World War II and the National Liberation Struggle.

The previously suppressed theme of the post-war killings made a sudden and unstoppable rise to the surface in the 1980s and 1990s, and it started to shift popular perceptions of the past by instilling widespread doubt about the entire history of World War II and the post-war period. The analysis of newspaper reports also demonstrates the old heroic imagery of World War II slowly being displaced, and the imagery of the post-war killings moving to centre stage, steadily reducing the history of World War II to the killings during and after the war.

Over the following decades, revisionist news discourses gained further momentum, and after 2000 it also gained in legitimacy, with material evidence such as the discovery of mass graves. The former media silence on the post-war killings was presented as a lie and mass deception – and, if this was a lie, it was concluded that everything else relating to World War II must be called into question as well. The discovered mass graves were, ironically, brought forth as the sole material evidence from World War II, and all other important war-related facts were flatly ignored. If one only looks at *Delo's* material published between 2005 and 2012, one finds that the most frequent representation of the Liberation Front of the Slovenian Nation was associated with the rift between the Partisans and the Home Guard. In such representations, the division between the Partisans and the foreign Axis forces (the Fascists and Nazis) was consigned to oblivion. The discursive frame devised by such a revisionist news discourse was based on prioritizing the domestic civil war.

As the analysis demonstrates, the vast majority of reports on World War II provide extremely sensationalist descriptions of Home Guard troops being killed at the hands of the Partisans, of mass graves being discovered, and of national reconciliation, thereby reducing the discourse of World War II to defining the

---

25 M. A., "Za povojne poboje kriva prejšnja oblast," *Delo*, 25 September, 1996, p. 1; see also Matjaž Albreht, "Za večino je vmesno poročilo sprejemljivo," *Delo*, 25 September, 1996, p. 2.

roles of executioners (the Partisans) and their victims (the Home Guard). Such a discursive framework builds on a story of the Partisans committing mass murders during and after the war. To quote one example, "This report [on post-war killings] contributes to continuing the dialogue on overcoming the burdens of totalitarian regimes."[26] The Partisan regime during World War II is suddenly embedded in the framework of a totalitarian regime. Reports began to feature personal accounts from living Home Guard members or their descendants, searching for witnesses in place of the missing documentary evidence.[27] Based on the large number of identified mass graves of collaborationist troops at the time, one report in *Delo* even speculated that Slovenia was perhaps "the largest post-war scaffold," and that at least 100,000 people had been killed after the war.[28] Most reports consistently argued that the communist leadership had long concealed not only the killings, but also the suffering of people who had lost family members and friends as a result.[29] What such reporting effectively does is to absolve them of their Fascist and Nazi collaboration, negate their military role during World War II, and portray them as nothing more than suffering civilian victims. *Delo* began to seek out new war victims, and in this discursive shift converted Partisan resistance against the Italian and German forces into aggression against ordinary people.[30] Forgiveness, tolerance, and national reconciliation were highlighted – however, it was exclusively directed at collaborationist actors, namely the Home Guard troops, and no forgiveness was granted to the Partisans for their post-war killings.[31] Within such a narrative framework, the revisionist news discourse blurs the boundaries between Stalinist methods and post-war killings in Slovenia and, as a result, subjects the entire Partisan engagement to being interpreted as an element of the worst kind of communist repression. As the analysis shows, the post-war killings then came to be suddenly viewed as an act of revenge by the Partisans, who were completely equated with the communists. In such a revisionist news discourse, the concept of "totalitarian regime" is employed as synonymous with the Partisan movement and communist Yugoslavia. Perpetuated by the media, such imagery also adds to deepening polarization and hatred among people.

Many other themes associated with World War II are being either ignored or tied to the civil war, and reduced to the division of the Partisans versus the Home

---

26 Matjaž Albreht, "Povojni poboji niso več tabu," *Delo*, 15 October, 2008, p. 4.
27 Dušan Grča, "Živ spomin na žrtve povojnih pobojev," *Delo*, 12 November, 2008, p. 4.
28 Jože Dežman, "Slovenija največje povojno morišče," *Delo*, 19 March, 2008, p. 2.
29 Matjaž Albreht, "Pozornost do ljudi, katerih trpljenje je (bilo) prikrito," *Delo*, 11 December, 2007, p. 2.
30 Matjaž Albreht, "Novi pogovori o žrtvah vojnega nasilja," *Delo*, 25 January, 2008, p. 2.
31 Špela Žabkar, "Predsednik Türk pozval k odpuščanju, strpnosti, spravi," *Delo*, 14 January, 2008, p. 2.

Guard, which means that all specific events and actors are interpreted through this lens. Everything related to World War II is implicitly relativized, and all victims of World War II are suddenly treated as equal. The victim discourse, extolling the Home Guard, moulds readers' perceptions in a way that arouses a sense of pity towards them. However, such pity is not only directed at the Home Guard: they sympathize with all erstwhile aggressors and feel especially deeply for all those who were killed during World War II, whereas the Partisans have suddenly come to be viewed as aggressors. News reports deepening the discursive break in the debate surrounding World War II provide audiences with specific imagery, and instruct them on how to sympathize with both belligerent sides in World War II. More specifically, the meaning of World War II is reduced to the issue of wartime violence and post-war killings, with absolutely no regard paid towards who was primarily responsible for the war's outbreak. This question has become completely irrelevant. In such news narratives, it is only the Partisans and the Liberation Front – now completely equated with the Communist Party – that are implicitly represented as the central culprits for all the human rights violations committed during and after the war.

Another effect of such revisionist news reporting is that it obscures all historical complexities, and thereby utterly fails to come to terms with the most obvious fact of what World War II was in the first place. The audiences, confronted with specific, entirely decontextualized details of the post-war killings, do not only find this problematic, but hardly even notice it, being fully immersed in the story of the Partisan executioners and the Home Guard troops as their victims. *Delo*'s narratives utterly fail to provide a wider context of World War II as characterized by total warfare and Nazi atrocities. For this reason, while the news discourse highlights a spate of specific narrations regarding the Home Guard troops who were executed, it completely ignores their collaboration with the Nazis. Similarly, almost no voice is given to actors who might provide answers concerning collaboration.

A detailed analysis of the vocabulary, and the use of words and names for various groups of soldiers fighting in World War II, reveals that those killed by the Partisans are consistently labelled "civilians" or "victims." In some cases, there is no indication whatsoever that these were Home Guard troops or other individuals who collaborated with the German forces and fought against the Partisans. They are often simply described as "victims of war crimes" or even "victims of the Partisans" or "victims of the communists." The Partisans, on the other hand, are given labels that discredit, dehumanize, and demonize them absolutely. The repeated use of phrases such as "Partisan slaughterers," "war criminals," "communist revolutionaries," or even "murderers," assigns collective guilt to one side only. The entire Partisan movement is criminalized primarily because it remains under-researched, and represented exclusively through the lens of the oppressive, totalitarian, and criminal communist regime. There seems to be total amnesia concerning the Tehran Conference of 1943, at which the Allied leaders officially recognized the Partisans as the only anti-fascist organization in the Yugoslav region. What such media revisionism, then, effectively does is to treat the Partisans on the same level as the Nazis, identifying the main aggressor in World War II not in Nazism, but in communism. The aim of such media revisionism is to shift the burden of responsibility away from Nazi collaborators by describing them as the victims of the Partisans, the communists, or even the Nazi leaders – but never as aggressors. To borrow a phrase from Miklavž Komelj, *Delo's* discourse completely deprives the Partisan movement of its revolutionary potential in order to serve the mythological construction of the Slovenian nation and the purposes of local fascism.[32] Media representations criminalizing the Partisan movement and extolling domestic collaborators as anti-communist national patriots not only permit the spread of vigorous historical revisionism within Slovenian public space, but also slowly transform the collective memory of the Slovenian nation.

Bottom-up memories: people's knowledge about World War II on two shores

What makes memory unique, according to Olick, is that it is in constant dialogue with the past.[33] From this vantage point, Slovenia may be considered "a natural laboratory for the study of collective memory."[34] Investigating the creation of memory from the bottom-up helps in understanding how different popular memories come together in public space, and how they coexist and struggle to assert a hegemonic position, and a dominant interpretation of the past. The

---

32 See, for example, Komelj, "The Function of the Signifier 'Totalitarianism'." The reinterpretation of the history of World War II, however, is a wider post-Yugoslav phenomenon, with other republics of the former Yugoslavia also confronting the emergence of vigorous revisionism. See also Ljiljana Radonic, "Croatia: Exhibiting Memory and History at the 'Shores of Europe'," *Culture Unbound: Journal of Current Cultural Research* 3 (2011): 355–367; Jovana Mihajlović Trbovc and Tamara Pavasović Trošt, "Who Were the Anti-Fascists? Divergent Interpretations of WWII in Contemporary Post-Yugoslav History Textbooks," in *The Use and Abuse of Memory: Interpreting World War II in Contemporary European Politics*, edited by Christian Karner and Bram Mertens (New Brunswick: Transaction Publishers, 2013), 173–191; Tea Sindbaek, "The Fall and Rise of a National Hero: Interpretations of Draža Mihailović and the Chetniks in Yugoslavia and Serbia since 1945," *Journal of Contemporary European Studies* 17 (2009) 1: 47–59.
33 See, e.g., Jeffrey K. Olick, "Genre Memories and Memory Genres: A Dialogical Analysis of May 8th, 1945 Commemorations in the Federal Republic of Germany," *American Sociological Review* 64 (1999) 3: 381–402.
34 Wertsch, "The Narrative Organization of Collective Memory," 124.

current confusion in Slovenia in terms of understanding the war and post-war events can only be fully grasped if one examines all the different kinds of bottom-up memories, contrasting them with institutionalized top-down memories, which aggressively spread revisionism and seek to effect a forced forgetting of this period. Projecting Wertsch's description of the Russian example onto the Slovenian one, it can be said that "this setting has witnessed a transition from strict, centralized control over collective memory to open, if not chaotic public debate and disagreement, and the result is that it provides examples of an unusually wide range of collective memory forms."[35]

Based on the informants' accounts and their discordant stories about the war and post-war developments, one may describe the current situation in Slovenia as extremely chaotic. The analysis of bottom-up memories shows how different memories become manifest in Slovenian public space, and also how they come face-to-face with the institutionalized top-down narratives of this past. When the strict, state-controlled collective memory of World War II was destabilized after the disintegration of Yugoslavia, a host of different memories came to light, and particularly those that were previously suppressed. As a result, there is now an open confrontation of different – even contested – memories in public space.

Although a broad national consensus regarding these past themes is yet to be reached, popular memory shows that people are confused about how they should now look at the past. This is evident from the respondents' accounts, which convey their personal experiences of World War II from different sides. On the one hand, some informants have started to speak openly about memories they kept locked in the intimacy of their private spheres under the former regime, as they stated. Aggressive campaigning by the right-wing political regime, which has been making vocal statements about the Partisans' wartime and post-war killings of the Home Guard troops since the 1990s, also prompted the informants in this study to speak up about their experiences and memories. As an analysis of their testimonies shows, the counter-memories, after having been suppressed under the former regime, are now successfully challenging the once-dominant collective memory. To provide one such example:

> In the past, or still today, you couldn't tell the truth about what happened. My father went to a Home Guard outpost and enlisted in the organization. And he was there, I don't know how long for. He came home when the war ended, went into hiding for three to four months, and finally decided to surrender. There was an amnesty for him. An American amnesty. Otherwise they killed everyone that surrendered. They took them to Kočevje Rog and killed them there. But my father was not in prison. Nowadays, the whole Slovenian nation is being lied to about what really happened. We should compare how many they killed, where they killed them, and how they killed them. But we were

---

35 Ibid.

always stigmatized. My brother wanted a job and the man who was supposed to sign his papers first asked him where his father was during the war. And he told him he didn't meet the employment conditions. And they accused us of such things. Now they are afraid to tell the truth and they can't tell the truth because all the documents have been destroyed. Mitja Ribičič was the man in charge of the killings. When he was summoned to court, he said "I don't know anything." And it was OK. But those who were with the White Guard – they treated them horribly during their interrogation. This is an injustice. It's not that I'm glorifying Hitler, maybe Hitler himself was wrong too, but the German people supported him. The communists are to blame for everything.
(male informant, 75 years old)

The quote above is just one in a spate of examples testifying to what is currently unfolding in Slovenian society – vigorous institutionalized, top-down revisionism, going hand-in-hand with increasingly vocal personal memories, which are surfacing after decades of silence. All these institutional discourses, and personal memories that were silenced for years, are struggling to produce a new regime of memory. They aim to redefine the historical significance of the Partisan movement and World War II, as well as to rehabilitate the Home Guard. Moreover, especially in southern parts of Slovenia (the Dolenjska region), where the Home Guard movement was strongest during World War II, such personal memories still strongly persist, and are in many cases also transmitted to younger generations through familial ties:

> We talked very little about this, because people were afraid. In the Dolenjska region, where I was born and lived, there were a lot of Home Guards, who were seen as very hostile by the government of that time. The less we talked about it, the better it was for us, but if we talked about it, we talked about it inside, in the intimacy of our homes.
> (female informant, 78 years old)

The stronger the personal memory of the inter-war and post-war killings, the stronger it is tied to revisionist discourses in Slovenia, and such counter-memories of Home Guards as victims vigorously clash with the previously dominant memories of Partisans as victims. This produces a chaotic situation in Slovenia, and in many cases most people are confused regarding how the history of World War II might be understood. I offer another example of such a counter-memory:

> Our family has experience of the killings – ten of my aunts and uncles. They took them into the caves and shot them. For a long time, we didn't know where their bodies were. In 2015, we found out about this cave in a hill near Hruševo. Then we buried their bones. I think children should learn about this in school. Younger generations should come face-to-face with everything – World War II as well as the post-war killings.
> (female informant, 82 years old)

I chose these examples to show how such personal memories, which rose to the surface after years of silence, go hand-in-hand with the ever louder institutional voices speaking of the post-war killings. Although about one-fifth of the respondents' accounts are consistent with such an interpretation, these counter-memories clash with the glorification of the Partisan past under the former regime, which also set out a clear distinction as to who the aggressor was, and who the victims were in World War II. Within this new politics of memory, when these roles are suddenly becoming blurred, and counter-memories are slowly taking on a hegemonic position, the role of the Axis aggressors, and of Hitler himself, is becoming relativized as well. It is the influence of such a memory regime that made one informant even question whether Hitler was right or not, before placing the blame for all the evil that occurred in World War II not on Hitler and Nazism, but on communism. These kinds of memories, as evoked by the informants, rehabilitate Nazism, and relativize the meaning of World War II by suddenly identifying the actual historical aggressor as the victim.

Such popular counter-memories, which are now rising to the surface, have started to alter the memory regime in such a way that even justifies totalitarian regimes such as Hitler's Nazism by maintaining that all mass-killings should be treated equivalently. Nevertheless, many of the informants still swear by historical interpretations of the Partisans as victims, but they are extremely confused by interpretations of the past that vilify the Partisans. In other words, such top-down interpretations are not congruent with their own experiences and memories, nor with the deeply rooted knowledge of World War II that they have acquired either at home or at school under the former regime. Moreover, these revisionist discourses and counter-memories are so aggressive as to leave the majority of the informants not only confounded but also doubting certain historical facts regarding World War II. This, for instance, is most evident from their admitted inability to clearly determine who the aggressor was, and who the liberator was. Furthermore, an analysis of the informants' testimonies shows that they even apologize for remembering the Partisans as the victims. Precisely this is the result of the new memory regime that is slowly taking shape in Slovenian society. To quote a few examples – from different generations – of how the once-dominant memory is struggling against the increasingly prevailing counter-memory, and how it is constantly seeking to justify its position:

> I don't know who to believe today. The Germans were the aggressors, the Partisans were the liberators. That's a sure bet, I think. At school, they taught us that the Home Guard was against the country. But the media today are attacking the picture we acquired in primary school. I can tell between facts and the interpretation of those Partisan traitors. The Partisans' role should be stressed more today. On the one hand, they say that Trieste was liberated by the Partisans, but, on the other, they claim that people had to flee from the Partisans. So, in my opinion, they talk too much about the Home Guard and not its

victims, the Partisans, they don't talk enough about the Partisans. I think the debate on the post-war killings has been blown out of proportion to promote certain people and political options. The media should place more of an emphasis on World War II, they should talk more about concentration camps and the spirit of that period, which was very cruel. I'm afraid that the younger generations know less and less about that period. I think it's a dangerous thing, to forget about World War II, because I really don't want it to repeat itself.
(female informant, 55 years old)

When I remember World War II, these were the years of fear, darkness, and denial. In our village, first there were Italians and later Germans. We could not walk freely outside of the village, there were controls everywhere. We children served as a link with the Partisans. Our parents sewed messages into the waists of our trousers or into some hidden part of a dress. If I think about the kind of danger we were in, a shiver goes down my spine. It is sad that we forget about the Partisans' suffering, I never felt that the war was inside the country, but was rather resistance to the occupiers. So, I feel sad, when today they worship the Home Guards and try to place them side by side with the Partisans.
(female informant, 84 years old)

From the very beginning, our family was a member of a liberation or Partisan army. Also, my mother's brother was among the first Partisans in the places where we lived. Nowhere in the world do they build monuments for enemy collaborators and they do not glorify them. Nowhere in the world do they belittle our liberators.
(female informant, 75 years old)

The majority of my respondents, from the middle-aged and older generation, agreed with the once-dominant memory of the Partisans as the liberators and victims of WWII, but what is interesting is that those who have personal experiences of WWII and personal memories of it (the older generation) are far more critical of present-day revisionism than those from the middle-aged generation, who in many cases doubt the once-dominant collective memory. This testifies to the fact that without personal experiences, the respondents are more likely to succumb to the revisionist discourses. Although they have strong testimonies from their parents, they are subjected to revisionist discourses that slowly attack their familial and school (mediated) memories. However, respondents from all generations justify in some way their belief in the Partisans, and this results from their bottom-up memory colliding with top-down revisionist discourses.

This is how struggles for the meaning of the Partisan and Home Guard Movements, the post-war killings, and World War II in general – struggles taking place both within top-down institutionalized memories and in publicly voiced personal memories – are becoming inscribed in the present-day collective memory of the Slovenian nation. As a result, the divide between the Partisans and the Home Guard (and the Nazis), which essentially marked the Slovenian people during World War II, is now being perpetuated even by generations without any direct experience of that period. For many informants, the memory battle over the divide between the Partisans and the Home Guard also underscores their current political position on the left–right axis. Nonetheless, it may be concluded with certainty that most informants, particularly those who grew up under the former regime, still remember the Partisans in an explicitly positive way. Following Slovenia's secession from Yugoslavia, the voices of opposition grew louder, and destabilized the meaning of the triumphant Partisan Movement of World War II. Under the influence of such revisionism, despite people's positive experiences of the Partisan resistance, many are also having second thoughts about how they should remember the Partisans now that counter-memories and revisionist discourses have become firmly embedded within memory schemata in Slovenia.

Moreover, the situation is even more complex and chaotic, as among the interviews I also found a few cases of personal experiences with compulsory mobilization in the German Army. Such counter-memories, which also do not comply with the previous dominant collective memory, or moreover, with memories of those who were on neither side during the war, cause additional confusion in the memory landscape of World War II Slovenia. For example:

> I have knowledge of World War II from school, while I was in school in socialist times, history classes placed an emphasis on World War II then. But I also know of it from the personal experiences of my parents. My father was mobilized in the German Army as a 20 year old boy and he served as an officer in neighbouring Austria. We did not sing any patriotic songs at home. I am sorry that the media nowadays want to show those organizations and people, who collaborated with the occupying forces, as patriotic Slovenians, but this still does not mean that I support people who killed all those innocent people after the war in a very ugly way. Those who were unfortunately, in many cases even though not through any fault of their own, on the wrong side.
> (female informant, 51 years old)

The key question that emerges here is that of what can be done in a society witnessing a clash between such conflicting memories, where personal memories are even contradictory to the extent that persons can no longer be certain of whether those memories refer to the same historical event. The accounts provided by the above informants confirm that the landscape of memories relating to World War II in Slovenia is extraordinarily diverse and multidimensional, with a flurry of different memories competing with one another. Alongside this, one must be mindful of the fact that the complexity of this situation also owes much to what the issue of traumatic memories addresses, because World War II was profoundly traumatic for all sides involved. As various competing memories bear witness:

After the war, the German Army and Home Guard took all the blame, as if they, the Partisans, had done everything right. Much was said about the Germans and their wrongdoings. Yet all everyone did was fight for freedom. When my father returned home and some men came to visit him and they talked, he always warned me to keep my mouth shut. They'd shoot him on the spot. There was discrimination at school as well. Those who were left-oriented were made more welcome, and we who were right-oriented became more marginalized – there was no help from the Red Cross or such for us. We were scum, inferior... The school had a kitchen and only the left-oriented pupils got something to eat. As for the rest of us from the village, we didn't get any food at school. We were all pro-right in our village, there were no Partisans. The Partisans concealed their sins for fifty, sixty years, and only now has this become public, how many killings there were. God forbid should you mention anything about this before. Once I said to a co-worker who was a party secretary, "do you know what the Partisans did after the war?" He told me, "hush, don't talk about this, someone might hear you." They knew everything, but this was a forbidden topic. They even killed before the war. My father told me that the Partisans came to steal things and didn't bother working. They came, dragged you into the woods, and killed you. This went on even before the war. But when the war was over, the OZNA came, that's an army, the special police. They killed someone from the neighbouring village; he was in the field when they came. And they shot him. No one could help him. (male informant, 74 years old)

I was in a concentration camp for four years. It was mostly humiliation, famine. I was still a child. It was very hard. All we did was wait for the moment when we could go home. Today, the right-wingers talk as if we were on vacation rather than in a concentration camp. They collaborated with Hitler and only pushed themselves to the front. The Home Guard and the White Guard, who collaborated with the Axis forces, are not telling the truth today about World War II. No one ever mentions that we were hungry, humiliated, beaten ... they have forgotten about this. The Partisans only wanted to free Slovenia, but the Home Guard aimed to destroy the Slovenes and sided with the Germans. I respect the Partisans, I have no respect for the Home Guard. We knew these people were in cahoots with the Axis forces; they betrayed their own people. (female informant, 83 years old)

What is striking, as the analysed interviews show, is the observation that the middle-aged generation have been much more subjected to top-down revisionist discourses, since they have no personal experiences nor personal memories of World War II, and are mostly dependent on transmitted memories. They only possess mediated memories (family, school, media etc.) of World War II, and in such a situation it is more likely that their memories become subject to the strong institutionalized top-down revisionist discourses that circulate in society, in contrast with the older generation who have personal experiences of World War II.

Both sides in the continuing divide, as the above statements illustrate, have embraced the institutionalized memory battle in the present-day public sphere in Slovenia. Popular memory is divided, and this division is part of popular memory schemata, as is further demonstrated by the informants' use of vocabulary, which points to the still ongoing battle between the two sides (e.g. "traitors," "liberators," "aggressors," "killers," "murderers," etc.). Hatred, antagonisms, and anger have become the key regulatory mechanisms that shape the memory of World War II, instead of tolerance, understanding, and appeasement. Drawing on Olick's diachronic model of memory, however, it can be concluded that the current situation regarding memory conflicts in Slovenia is only a phase in the evolution of memory because collective memory develops through history rather than remaining static.[36] Current collective memories regarding World War II, as the analysed cases show, is chaotic and complexly divided. The analysed politics of memory from the bottom-up testifies to the present memory regime, which is based on interpretive pluralism (of different co-existing memories) and divided memories, and not on a consensual collective memory.

Conclusion

The analysis of *Delo*'s politics of remembering and popular memories through personal accounts shows that the deep-rooted Yugoslav collective memory of World War II and the subsequent dominant media interpretations of the war and post-war developments were first destabilized in the late 1980s, and seriously undermined in the 1990s. The old media imagery of World War II and of old memories became part of the new politics of remembering; a politics premised on revisionism and memory transformation, and subjected to the ideological dictate of minimizing and trivializing the importance of the Partisans as liberators, and of the totality of experiences relating to World War II. This is the same ideological dictate that, on the other hand, accentuates and glorifies the importance of the civil war, the post-war killings, and the Home Guard. Institutionalized top-down narratives, such as media images in *Delo*, now fortify those places of memory that equate Nazism with communism and, instead of the victims of the Axis powers, above all commemorate the victims of totalitarian regimes (primarily of communism, and the Home Guard troops as the victims of the Communist Partisans).

Opinion polls in Slovenia[37] testify that memory schemata have slightly changed among Slovenian people over the years. Although the percentage of

---

36 Olick, Jeffrey K. *The Politics of Regret: On Collective Memory and Historical Responsibility*, New York, 2007.
37 Toš, "Vrednote v prehodu".

those positively evaluating the Home Guards has been increasing, the Partisans are still far more positively evaluated than the Home Guards. However, the results of such opinion polls in a way may show that the ideological dictate of *Delo* in Slovenian society is not as powerful as one would presuppose. The Partisan legacy, on the other hand, is still very strong in Slovenia, and we can talk about the wartime resistance as a positive Partisan memory, which in a way relativizes *Delo's* discourse and weakens its ideological dictate. The resistance as a positive Partisan memory is also visible in the results of my empirical study of bottom-up memory. To summarize the results, I can divide the informants' testimonies and memories into four groups: 1) those insisting on positive Partisan memories, 2) positive Home Guards' memories and a revisionist refusal of group one's memories, 3) a kind of confusion surrounding positive Partisan memories (these three groups are in the majority), 4) positive Partisan memories and a critical refusal of Home Guards' memories and present revisionist tensions in Slovenia (this group constitutes a minority of informants' answers). In general terms, there are many more memories that deal with the Partisans as liberators, victims and positive figures, but my results testify that also these strong positive Partisan memories are slowly being transformed, while many of these respondents have asked themselves how to interpret World War II, namely which side was bad and which side was good, who was the liberator and who the aggressor etc. Despite cultivating positive memories of the Partisans, many informants found themselves in somewhat of a dilemma over how to define the Partisans in such a complex memory landscape. And this may be precisely the effect of strong anti-Partisan and pro-Home Guard public debate in Slovenia, also produced in the media, e.g. in *Delo*. The results of this study thus partly raise doubts concerning the results of opinion polls, while informants, however, rate the Partisans very highly, but do not know how to "correctly" interpret and understand their role in the Second World War. This is a product of different ideological discourses circulating in Slovenia that try to demonize the Partisans (with *Delo* among them).

However, on the other hand, the revisionist politics of remembering, thus sows fear and strife among people as well as spreading contempt and aversion towards the Partisan resistance as a national liberation movement. Vilified media images of the Partisans and communism, equated with Nazism, have become an integral part of both top-down media narratives and an increasingly integral part of personal accounts – that is, popular memory. Collaboration is being commemorated and collaborators are being represented as real Slovenian nationalists that collaborated with the Nazi forces for the sole purpose of resisting another totalitarian regime – communism. Such stances seek to justify collaboration with the Nazis by portraying the communists as far worse criminals. In this way, communism is treated on a par with Nazism, and the post-war killings in Slovenia are interpreted as exemplifying the most atrocious, Stalinist-style reprisals perpetrated by the Partisans. According to Radonic, responsibility for equating red and black totalitarianisms, and therein also the aggressively perpetuated revisionist politics of the past, also lies with EU politics: "Thus, not only has the memory of the victims of Stalinism been added to the European canon, but furthermore, the victims of both regimes have also been explicitly placed on the same level."[38]

As an ideological apparatus and an institutional media arena manipulating images of the past, *Delo* plays a highly ambiguous role by presenting difficult moments of the past through the construction of divisions and trauma. According to Zelizer, mediated images of the past could form new individual experiences among people, spread empathy, and treat memory as a social issue,[39] which *Delo* does not do. Thus, the revisionist media discourse is creating not only dominant images of the recent past but also new divisions as well as new cultural and historical values, stances, and beliefs, which legitimate the new politics of memory and truth.

Furthermore, the discussion of the Partisans and the Home Guard has also led to the construction of a whole new memory landscape in Slovenia, divided between positive and negative memories of the Partisans. As the memory analysis shows, there are no clearly defined roles of the Nazi aggressor and the Partisan liberator in the divided memory schemata present in Slovenian society. It is here, at the intersection of top-down and bottom-up memories, that it becomes most clear how cultural and political tensions in the present determine and mould collective memory and history, because "present conditions shape the selective memory of past events."[40] The forced forgetting of World War II and the Partisan movement, as promoted by the media discourse, is also reflected in the informants' bottom-up memories. Zemon Davis and Starn warn: "To forget the past wilfully is to threaten the fragile links that, however tenuously, guard us from oblivion."[41] This is because such forgetting and the transformation of memory makes possible a surge of new forms of non-consensual collective memory based on the conflict between the forced forgetting of the Partisan movement and pro-Partisan interpretations of the past.

---

38 Radonic, "Croatia," 360.
39 Barbie Zelizer, "Finding Aids to the Past: Bearing Personal Witness to Traumatic Public Events," in *Media Anthropology*, edited by Eric W. Rothenbuhler and Mihai Coman (Thousand Oaks: Sage, 2005), 199–200, 199–209.
40 Corcoran, "The Political Instrumentality of Cultural Memory," 61.
41 Natalie Zemon Davis and Randolph Starn, "Introduction," *Representations* 26 (Special Issue: Memory and Counter-Memory) (1989): 6, 1–6.

Oto Luthar

The Sanitation of Slovenian Post-Socialist Memorial Landscape

Introduction

Furthering the analyses[1] of changes in the post-socialist memorial landscape in Slovenia after 1991, this article focuses on the latest shift in this process, which, more than anything to date, also points to changes in the post-socialist historiographical narrative. While the first twenty years following the end of socialism were marked by the revisionist ambition to redistribute responsibility (and blame) for collaboration with occupying forces by placing the responsibility squarely on the Slovenian Partisans, the memorials built after 2014 seek a more radical reinterpretation. According to inscriptions on the last generation of the so-called parish plaques[2] that were erected from the mid-2010s onward, the

---

1 The contribution is a tentative synthesis of research conducted so far into post-socialist revision of the historical interpretation of the Second World War and the socialist period. The research encompasses the gathering of information on changes in the memorial landscape (from the desecration of Partisan and Jewish monuments to erecting monuments to "victims of communist violence"), on commemorations held at the sites of postwar executions of Fascist and Nazi collaborators, as well as the analysis of changes in the school curriculum. Partial results have been published in a number of journals ("Forgetting Does (Not) Hurt" in *Nationalities Papers*, Vol. 41, 2013; "Changes in the Post-Socialist Memorial Landscape and the Notion of the Civil War in Slovenia" in *Slovene Studies*, Vo. 40, No 1–2, 2018) and the books "Post-Socialist Historiography Between Democratization and New Exclusivist Politics of History," edited by Oto Luthar; *Of Red Dragons and Evil Spirits. The Post-Communist Historiography Between Democratization and New Politics of History* (Budapest: CEU Press, 2017); "Memory, Revision, Resistance: Reviving the Partisan Monuments along the Slovenian-Italian Border" in Borut Klabjan (ed.), *Borderlands of Memory. Adriatic and Central European Perspectives* Berlin: Lang, 2019), and were presented at two conferences, the first organized by the ASEES –Association for Slavic East European & Eurasian Studies, and the second by the ASN-Association for the Study of Nationalities in New York.
2 The term parish plaques in reference to the Home Guard monuments was introduced by a group of people who organized the installation of the monuments in parish cemeteries in central Slovenia. They included among them some active members of the collaborating Home Guard units established under the Nazi command after the capitulation of Italy. As the plaques were placed on the chapels of parish cemeteries, the term refers to factual locations. What

Partisans and civilian victims of the Nazi and Fascist occupation are being transformed into perpetrators, whereas the members of collaborationist units organized as Home Guards are being praised as members of the "Slovenian National Army."³

The first part of the analysis, however, looks into US involvement in this process. In 2014, Joseph A. Mussomeli, the former US ambassador to Slovenia, initiated the installing of a commemorative plaque that describes Nazi and Fascist collaborators as "Slovenians [...] who sought peace but could not avoid war."⁴ In so doing, this plaque not only reinterpreted the most traumatic part of modern Slovenian history, but also became directly involved in the Slovenian politics of the past.

To understand the consequences of this involvement, one should be familiar with the general changes in the Slovenian memorial landscape and the influence of Home Guard⁵ monuments that have been erected after 1991. Not least because this was, and still is, a unique practice all across post-socialist Europe. Therefore, the new memorial sites in post-socialist Slovenia are not just sites for commemoration and for a new politics of the past, but also sites of trauma. And the extent to which they remain invested with trauma marks the extent to which memory has not effectively come to terms with it. This is why the new memorials

---

remains unclear is the connection between the initiators and local communities. In any event, the installation of the plaques evoked both support and contention at the same time. Some supporters were not satisfied with the politicization of the project, while others were interested in an even more direct confrontation with (if present) the existing partisan monuments.

3 According to the Slovenian Cardinal Franc Rode, the "real national traitors were the communists," who forced the Nazi and Fascist collaborators "to start the counter-revolution." From the Letter of the Slovenian Alternative Academy; source: STA (Slovenska tiskovna agencija – Slovenian Press Agency), July 13, 2016.

4 Besides transforming the perpetrators into victims, the deputy ambassador invited the audience gathered in front of the embassy in August 2016 "to honor and celebrate" the Slovenian negationists as "those who honestly seek reconciliation" and "strive to preserve Slovenia's independence and identity." The whole inscription on the plaque, entitled *"In Remembrance of All Victims of Totalitarian Regimes,"* reads as follows: *"We honor and grieve for all Slovenes who suffered under fascism and Nazism; We honor and grieve for all Slovenes who suffered under communism; We honor all Slovenes who sought peace and could not avoid war; We honor and celebrate those brave Slovenes who seek reconciliation; We celebrate all Slovenes who fight to preserve Slovenia's independence and identity; We celebrate the courage, compassion, and decency of the Slovene people."*

5 The formal name of the Nazi collaborators in Slovenia is Domobranci. Domobranci, or Home Guard units, were formed immediately after Italy's capitulation in September 1943, although the first Home Guards swore allegiance in April 1944. In the ongoing discussion about the involvement of the Home Guard in supporting the Nazis, one should always look at the wording of the oath of allegiance, which contains a line that does not leave much room for interpretation, saying that this was merely a so-called "functional collaboration." See also Gregor J. Kranjc, *To walk with the devil. Slovene collaboration and Axis occupation, 1941–1945* (Toronto: University of Toronto Press, 2013).

can serve as a tool for understanding the so-called "semantic decoding" of heroes and victims. Although the conversion of the European heroic memorial landscape into a memorial landscape of victims took place earlier and before 1989, the end of socialism accelerated this process. The difference is that in Eastern Europe, most of the blame for the enormous losses of human life due to the Second World War was placed on communism, the revolution, and the resistance movement, which in the revisionist interpretation prompted the rise of a "counter" movement. The same holds true for the (re)interpretation of the US Embassy.

Misperceptions and Denial

Case Study I – The US Misperception

As already mentioned, the wording on the plaque installed on the US Embassy fence offers an interpretation in which the Nazi and Fascist collaborators are remembered and mourned as "Slovenians who sought peace" but "could not avoid war." Besides this, the plaque honours and celebrates all "those brave Slovenians who seek reconciliation," since they are the ones who "strive to preserve Slovenia's independence and identity."

Leaving aside the fact that in Slovenia, the reconciliation narrative is being used to score points in everyday political disputes wherein national reconciliation has been hijacked for revisionist purposes – as well as the US political, historiographical, and ideological agenda, I argue that the interpretation offered on the US Embassy's fence is more or less a part of the Slovenian revisionist politics of the past. Nevertheless, the dictum of "all who sought peace but could not avoid war" is identical to the interpretation of those who stand for the political rehabilitation of collaborators.

This also applies for the second part of the inscription, which celebrates those who honestly seek reconciliation. Since no representative of the Association of Veterans of the National Liberation Struggle has ever taken part in these commemorations, it seems reasonable to assume that in using the words cited above, the Embassy was probably not referring to the Partisans and other members of the resistance.

On the contrary, together with other initiators of the revisionist commemoration, the US mission ignores not only the historical facts,[6] but also the

---

6 According to Heinrich Himmler in his capacity as Reich Commissar for the Strengthening of Germandom, all "undesirable" Slovenes, meaning the majority of the intelligentsia and other "nationally conscious" Slovenes, were to be transferred to the Old Reich, Croatia or Serbia.

collaborators' distinctly pro-Nazi ideology, including anti-Semitism. From a Home Guard perspective, "the Partisans were drugged and bought by Jews in order to make them destroy the Slovenian nation, while on the side of the Slovenian Home Guard stands a German soldier fighting against the worldwide Jewry."[7] Similarly to in other parts of Central Europe, the fear of "Judeo-Communism" was also used in Slovenia as an alibi for the typical anti-Semitism of Slovenian collaborators ... And finally, the plaque ignores the fact that just as in Croatia, Serbia, Lithuania, Latvia, Estonia, Ukraine, Norway, etc., the local collaborators in Slovenia were integrated into the mechanisms of the mass murder of the Jews. They were not the ones who committed the murders, but they were accessories to murder, having gathered and handed over Jews and members of the resistance to the Germans who sent them to concentration camps in Germany and Poland.

Shortly after the installation of the plaque on the fence of the US Embassy, I wrote an article emphasizing this aspect of collaboration,[8] which met with little response. Apart from a critical comment by the Austrian-Slovenian historian Tamara Griesser Pečar from the Study Center for National Reconciliation,[9] and a

---

Thanks to the Partisan resistance, which started less than four months into the occupation, "only" 80,300 or about 5 % of the total Slovenian population instead of more than 200,000 people destined for deportation were sent to Croatia and Serbia, or into labour camps in Germany.

7 The Slovenian Home Guards claimed as late as 1945 that they "honestly [fought] side by side with Germany against the greatest enemy of humanity – communism" or "Jewish communism;" Doroteja Lešnik and Gregor Tomc, *Rdeče in črno. Slovensko partizanstvo in domobranstvo* (Ljubljana: Znanstveno in publicistično središče, 1995), 124.

8 Oto Luthar, "Razumevanje preteklosti: Presenetljivo? Ne. Nedopustno? Da." *Sobotna priloga Dela*, May 9, 2014. Also available at: http://www.delo.si/zgodbe/sobotnapriloga/razumevanje-preteklosti-presenetljivo-ne-nedopustno-da.html.

9 First (in 2005) established as the historical section of the Sector for the Redressing of Injustices and National Reconciliation, the Study Center for National Reconciliation started to operate within the framework of the Ministry of Justice. In 2008, the Government of the Republic of Slovenia founded it as an independent institute under its current name. According to the center's official website, "the reason for" its creation was "an objective need for [...] objective examination of historical facts and realization of the conditions for national reconciliation." The Government, whose member was also the husband of the director of the study centre, was interested in following "the footsteps of Central and East European countries (e.g. Germany, Poland, the Czech Republic, Lithuania, Latvia, Estonia, Slovakia, and Hungary), which have been through a similar historical experience to Slovenia." Although established as an "independent research institution," its members were and still are personally connected with leading conservative politicians aspiring towards a radical reinterpretation of the national history of the Second World War and the socialist period. Instead of "creating and implementing conditions for bringing into being national reconciliation among Slovenians," the members of the centre systematically ignore the role of the Partisan resistance by trying to rehabilitate collaborators with the Nazi and Fascist occupiers.

reflection on the article by Irena Šumi,[10] my writing received no further comments. Since there was also no response to my criticism from the US Embassy, I contacted the former ambassador, who initiated the installation of the plaque, and who is the new head of the diplomatic mission. After two years of waiting for a response, which was ultimately signed by the Embassy's public affairs officer, I was advised to once again contact the person who initiated the plaque's construction. However, given that the former ambassador also failed to respond to my second letter, I can only infer the mission's position from the letter sent to me by the public affairs officer in late March 2018.

In addition to the known facts about who initiated the plaque's construction and in what context, the letter only included a quote from the English part of the wording on permanent display on the plaque itself. Apart from this, the public affairs officer merely informed me that every year, the Study Center requests the Embassy to send a representative to greet them "during their annual activities associated with the European Day of Remembrance for Victims of Totalitarian Regimes."[11] The letter states nothing about the role of those mentioned on the plaque, and nothing about the former alliance between the Slovenian/Yugoslav Resistance and the Allied Forces.

The same holds for the speech[12] that the person behind the initiative for the plaque gave on the day of its installation. In his brief historical overview, Ambassador Mussomeli mentioned numerous events, from Pharaoh Thutmose III and the Battle of Megiddo, to the American Civil War, and the US invasion of Iraq. Yet he did not make one single mention of the people referred to on the commemoration plaque. He merely came up with the rhetorical question: "How dare we not honour and commemorate all those who have been victims of injustices perpetrated by both Rightist and Leftist regimes?" And instead of providing clear answers, Ambassador Mussomeli offered more generic statements such as "nothing is black-and-white," "history is more than just facts," and that life itself is more than a "Manichean struggle between absolute good and absolute evil." The ambassador's speech does, however, include several pieces of patronizing advice regarding history being "a fierce insistence on knowing the truth," which is not "possible without humility." He concluded with the recommendation that Slovenes pursue "true reconciliation," which will enable "real healing" to begin.

I received a rather similar answer from the Slovenian president Borut Pahor, whom I requested make a statement about the US plaque. As if in concordance

---

10 Irena Šumi, "Slovenski antisemitizem, živ pokopan v ideologiji slovenske narodne sprave," *Časopis za kritiko znanosti* 260 (2015): 69–84.
11 From the official letter written by the Public Affairs Officer of the Embassy of the United States of America.
12 The speech entitled "Totalitarianism and Reconciliation" was given by Ambassador Joseph A. Mussomeli on the day of the unveiling of the plaque, 16 April 2014.

with the US ambassador, he too decided not to answer my questions directly, but rather through his communication and public relations advisor. In almost complete accord with the statement of the US mission, the Slovenian presidency stressed that the Slovenes require national reconciliation. Even more so, according to his advisor's reply, the president believes that such reconciliation is only possible "through collaboration between various political forces" and that "authentic reconciliation" can be obtained with "small and discreet steps."[13] According to the President Pahor, the monument "on the fence of the US Embassy [...] is considered to be a monument of the territory of the American Embassy," which is why he does not view it as an undiplomatic interference in Slovenia's internal affairs. This is probably also the reason why he has never commented on the idea by Slovenian activists that the Slovenian mission in Washington should start with a one-sided annual commemoration of the Trail of Tears, i.e. of a series of forced relocations of the Native American population carried out by the US government and army.

Although he made explicit reference to "small and discreet steps," President Pahor has never much cared for them, especially when it came to the question of "national reconciliation." This is evidenced by his speech on the unveiling of a joint memorial in Velike Lašče,[14] which, despite protests from the Partisans' relatives, bears the names of both collaborators and members of the resistance movement. It is evidenced by the solemn inauguration of the monument to the Ustashe and their families who were killed after the war at Dobrava cemetery in Maribor.[15] And, finally, it is evidenced by the Monument to the Victims of All Wars, the erection of which Pahor negotiated, therein directly violating the "will of the citizens."[16]

Given that Marko Zajc deals with the latter monument in greater detail, let me only point to a few reactions to the president's insistence on building it. The vast majority of people feel that instead of "catharsis," "a strong point of contact," or a "minimal common denominator for identification," Pahor's "monument of love"[17] represents little else than "empty blocks of concrete," and a "lonely reminder of the memory lost."[18]

---

13 From the letter by the advisor to the President of the Republic of Slovenia, Borut Pahor, to the author, February 28, 2018.
14 Velike Lašče is a town 30 km south-east of Ljubljana. See also Mekina, Borut. "Zanikanje Holokavsta. Zakaj v Sloveniji zanikanje holokavsta ni kaznivo?", *Mladina*, May 12, 2017.
15 According to the official website of the Office of the President of the Republic, the president visited the new memorial on 3 October 2016.
16 Peter Kolšek, "Metafizika v avgustu," *Sobotna priloga Dela*, August 5, 2017, 32.
17 In his opening address, the president called the Monument of the Victims of All Wars "the monument of love."
18 Ibid.

Case Study II – the Denial of Anti-Monuments

Something similar holds true for the proponents seeking to erect a monument in Grahovo, a small town forty kilometres from Ljubljana. On the face of it, just as with the majority of "martyrs of the revolution" monuments, this one also completely ignores the Home Guards' anti-Semitism and shooting of hostages. What is more, just as with the US Embassy's memorial plaque, this monument does not really seek reconciliation, but strives for a complete reordering of traumatic memory. The only difference between the plaque at the US Embassy in Ljubljana and the monument for the Martyrs of the Revolution in Grahovo is that the anti-monument in Grahovo – which was deliberately erected in front of the already existing monument dedicated to the Partisans, hostages and other victims of Fascism and Nazism – unequivocally calls for a complete reversal of roles, portraying the members of the Liberation Front as "communists." The collaborating Home Guards, on the other hand, are presented as members of "the Slovenian National Army," waiting for the new "generation [to] break the… false silence" and restore their "stolen honour and truth."

In an attempt to present the rhetoric, symbolism and choreography involved in such initiatives, I was once again interested in the political agenda behind this and other revisionist monuments. By reversing the roles of victims and perpetrators, their creators and initiators not only aim to subvert the meaning of the resistance movement, collaboration and communism, but also to enable the ethnicization of suffering.

Colonizing the central positions of the cemetery and adapting the usual Christian symbols, routines and traditions, these new monuments perfectly blend into the existing memorial landscape. Similar to the red, five-pointed star in the mise-en-scène of monuments dedicated to the resistance movement and the revolution, the crucifix is the operative and central piece as well as the main decoration on monuments dedicated to the "victims/martyrs of communism." The same goes for the inscriptions, which also follow Christian liturgy. Besides the usual Christian phrases associated with the departure of loved ones, such as "rest in peace," there are frequent references to God as the supreme moral adjudicator or the sole source of consolation.[19] By becoming part of the liturgical commemoration, these monuments blend well into the cemetery's existing mise-en-scène. In becoming an essential part of the ordinary Christian commemorative routine, they have established themselves as an indispensable part of community life.

---

19 "Accept, oh Lord, my wounds, offered to Thee in my hour of death;" "…until we meet in the eternal homeland;" "I am the resurrection and the life;" "he who believes in Me shall live even if he dies."

The new Home Guard monuments, however, have also started to colonize public space beyond parish cemeteries. Through being installed in community centres and other public areas, they have changed not only in form and style, but have also started to convey a new message. In fact, they have started to act as counter-monuments, and have thus become instrumental in helping the revisionist narrative gain wider public support. Namely, not only do they present perpetrators as victims and transform the real victims into perpetrators, they also exclude the latter from the process of mourning. As a sort of counter-history (*Gegengeschichte*), as introduced by Peter Hallama and Stephan Stach,[20] memorials such as the Reconciliation Plaque and the Martyrs of the Revolution monument have been created to confront the existing memorial landscape, understood as a part of the previous (socialist/communist) master narrative. At the same time, they have also been created to support and strengthen the so-called "shield" theory, according to which the decision of some Slovenes to collaborate with the occupying forces shielded the nation from even greater repression from within.[21]

Advocates of this theory even claim that "the Slovenes still (live) in a totalitarian system"[22] contaminated by "Nazi-Communist-Fascism."[23] In the central revisionist journal *Zaveza*, the Partisans are continually presented as "executioners," who committed "genocide" and are now blocking the process of reconciliation. In their view, the last government proposal to build a monument to the victims of all wars is "just another manipulation."[24] According to *Zaveza*'s authors, true reconciliation can only be attained by erecting monuments dedicated to the Home Guards.[25] Anything else is a "hoax," a "lie," and an obstacle "in the search for lost empathy."[26]

---

20 Peter Hallama and Stepahn Stach, *Gegengeschichte: Zweiter Weltkrieg und Holocaust im ostmitteleuropäischen Dissens* (Leipzig: Leipzig Univerzitätsverlag, 2015).
21 The same arguments were used to justify political collaboration in France in the sense that collaboration had a moderating effect on the repercussions of the Nazi occupation. In Slovenia, as in France, historical facts point in a different direction. By far the gravest part of the occupation period, the deportation of Slovenes from Styria to slave labor, gives no indication that the Slovenian authorities opting for collaboration with the Italian and German occupying forces exerted any moderating influence. On the contrary: like in Vichy France, so too in Provincia di Lubiana, Italians did not even approve of arming Slovenian village guards (*vaške straže*). See also Gerhard Hirschfeld, "Collaboration in Nazi-Occupied France: Some Introductory Remarks," edited by Gerhard Hirschfeld and Patrick Marsh, *Collaboration in France. Politics and Culture during the Nazi Occupation, 1940–1944* (Oxford, New York, Munich: Berg, 1989).
22 Vanja Kržan, "Kdaj spravni spomenik?" *Zaveza* XXIV, no. 92, 2014, 65.
23 Pavel Ferluga, "TIGR in ideologija," *Demokracija*, July 14, 2016, 8.
24 Anton Drobnič, "Tri vrtnice," *Zaveza* XXIV, no. 92, 2014, 96.
25 Vanja Kržan, "Kdaj spravni spomenik?" *Zaveza* XXIV, no. 92, 2014, 65.
26 Jože Trontelj, "V iskanju izgubljenega sočutja," *Zaveza* XXIV, no. 92, 2014, 72.

Given that it has remained unchanged for over twenty-five years, the rhetoric of denial and the disqualification of authors who disagree[27] represents one of the crucial premises to understanding the transformation of the Second World War memory culture in Slovenia and elsewhere.

After excluding their victims and the victims of the Fascist and Nazi occupation, the revisionists present collaborators and their family members as a uniform group of victims of communist terror. In the final stage of this reinterpretation, the resistance against the occupying forces is also interpreted as a "communist revolution," which in revisionist opinion is equivalent to a war "against its own people."[28] But more important than this are (a) the complete de-subjectivization and (b) the utter disregard for the victims of the Nazi and Fascist terror, as well as the victims of the Home Guards. And most importantly, as in the case of Partisan monuments, whose aura has until recently been slowly fading away, the "victims" represented by the Home Guard monuments do not fit into the process of individual participation in different levels of society. In order to foster national unity, the major element connecting these types of memorials is their implicit or explicit political significance. Despite being a collection of names, these monuments are appropriated, used, claimed, and/or instrumentalized by persons other than immediate family and close friends. The relevance of these deaths is perceived as more important than the individual victims. By creating greater traumas, they become a public issue. Therefore, there are no individuals on the side of the relatives either, since the relatives lose control over the mourning and memorialization practices as well.[29]

Given the above, one can speak of a complete amnesia and determined unwillingness on the part of the new revisionists to acknowledge basic facts. Their narrative does not even include the victims of the Home Guards, let alone the acknowledgment of collaboration with the Nazis and Fascists in the transformed memorial landscape. What is more, the function of self-victimization is not only to run away from the responsibility of perpetrators, but to avoid any "politics of remorse."[30] What happened in Slovenia and other post-socialist countries after the fall of socialism followed closely the events in Austria immediately after the war and in Germany at the end of the 1970s, and during the early 1980s. What is

---

27 All those who disagree with the revisionist "post-communist" interpretation have lately been branded the "internal enemies" of the Slovenian nation. See Matjaž Gruden, "'Slovenski holokavst' ali kako manipulira zborovodja mopedšova za republiko," in *Fokuspokus*, August 29, 2018.
28 Jože Dežman, "Naj se zgodovina odpre" (Interview), *Mag* 9–10 (2003): 44–48.
29 See also Peter Jan Margry and Cristina Sánchez-Carretero, *Grassroots memorials. The politics of memorializing traumatic deaths* (New York: Berghahn Books, 2011).
30 Aleida Assmann, *Das neue Unbehagen an der Erinnerungskultur. Eine Intervention* (Munich: Beck Verlag, 2013), 148.

referred to as the *Engführung des Gedächtnisses* ("narrowing of memory") in Germany, may be regarded as historical amnesia in Slovenia. As a part of the culture of self-victimization in Slovenia, this is based not only on revision, but on a complete negation of historical facts. Therefore, the revisionist interpretation also allows for no trace of the "politics of regret" (Jeffrey Olick) and no real memory exchange for the time in Slovenian revisionist memory culture, only a competition of victimization. The same holds for Slovenian "dehistoricized historiography," which, according to Jacques *Rancière*,[31] is unable to pin down the reality of a certain event. Due to the radical reinterpretation of Slovenian revisionists (either historians or politicians), all those (historians and social scientists) who oppose the described transformation of perpetrators into victims have a problem with proving the reality of what happened. Even more so, by transmuting it into a Party hell, the Slovenian denial of collaboration disintegrates into the realism of "the politics of the possible," which, according to Rancière, must be taken seriously, because it is not an expression of the real. Rather, it is an "expression of the possible."

The operation that follows manifests itself through two non-separable symptoms. The first can be seen as an exclusion of the real, and the second is nothing but revisionism itself; revisionism that declares that what is not possible is not real. In trying to prove the impossibility of error on the part of Fascist and Nazi collaborators, its Slovenian version maintains that "it is not possible that fifty percent of the Slovenian nation could have lived in error."[32] Instead, they sought refuge under the wings of the occupying Nazi regime to fend off the danger of communism. The last chapter of this narrative brings forth extreme revisionist voices attempting to proclaim the activities of collaborators as "national-liberating and heroic."[33] The same interpreters equate the resistance movement across the board with communism, even though less than one tenth of its members were actually communists.

Three decades after the end of socialism/communism, one section of the post-socialist historiography (not to mention politics) in Slovenia has problems with the notion of not only what is real, but also what is true. Nevertheless, the radical reinterpretation, as stressed at the beginning, deliberately overlooks the collaborators' distinctly pro-Nazi ideology, including anti-Semitism. Whereas in the case of Slovenia, the glorification of the leader (Führer) was indeed replaced by the glorification of the "Fatherland" and "God," the attitude toward Jews, as

---

31 Jacques Rancière, "Über den Nihilismus in der Politik," edited by Rado Riha, *Politik der Wahrheit*, (Vienna: Turia + Kant, 1997), 130.
32 Draga Ahačič, *Osvobodilna ali državljanska vojna* (Ljubljana: Cankarjeva založba, 1992), 11.
33 Ibid.

manifest in anti-Semitic hate speech, remained the same: "Jews are out to enslave the world."[34]

Similar statements to those that have coloured the debates of Slovenian revisionists and their supporters[35] over the past five years help the analysis of changes in the memorial landscape retain their current relevance. This is one of the reasons why we cannot play down the importance of this process or its actors. Quite the opposite, now more than ever before, the revisionist approach wields its overarching influence on the fabrication of memory and the mystification of the past. And more so than any other method of historical interpretation, historical revisionism reflects a pre-elaborated choice of seeing. Striving to invent a history that can retrospectively justify the role of a certain political and/or ideological perspective, revisionist history-makers are not willing to move beyond the either/or-ism of objectivity – unless this interferes with their role in contextualizing agents. In this respect, revisionists are typical constructionists who, in telling us what the past means, lean on their political/ideological preferences. Borrowing Alun Munslow's vocabulary, I choose to stress that Slovenian revisionist historiography, as a typical representational way of making history, operates as a politically "initiated and directly controlled" system of argumentation, guided by a set of ontological pre-judgements.[36] For Slovenian historians who still (or once again) believe that to interpret history is to bring an ideological moral perspective to it, the (ideal) historian remains an omniscient, utterly unreflective narrator who is able to single out truthful answers to all complex historical problems.

On the other hand, the revisionist intervention made it clear that memory (either as a part of historical interpretation or as a part of popular representation) can only be understood as an actively produced representation, and is hence completely open to struggle and dispute. At the beginning of the twenty-first century, national identity in Slovenia is, much like in other post-socialist countries, largely formed through "places of memory," rather than through the concept of national identity understood in relation to the history of a "politically determined group of citizens." What is more, this shift, according to Susannah Radstone, "comprises a 'culturalization' as well as 'spatialization' of a previously

---

34 Lešnik and Tomc, *Rdeče in črno*, 123–124.
35 One of the central proponents of post-socialist anti-Semitism in Slovenia is Bernard Brščič, a former state secretary in the cabinet of the prime minister, who recently stated that "[t]he German nation is a victim of Jewish imposition and brain burning with so-called holocaustology," which is "a perfidious Jewish design to restrain the German mind [...] and devise a plan of de-Germanisation, de-Frenchisation and de-Britishisation [...] and create a multiculti dystopia," in Mekina, Borut. "Zanikanje holokavsta. Zakaj v Sloveniji zanikanje holokavsta ni kaznivo?" *Mladina*, May 12, 2017.
36 Alun Munslow, *The New History* (Harlow: Pearson Longman, 2003), 186 and 187.

politicized and temporalized national memory." Yet at the same time, the memorial landscape "continues to evoke 'the past' albeit a 'past' that is remembered through place and as a symbol of 'politically and historically inert memories'."[37] Accordingly, we have to question Zygmunt Bauman's premise that "modernity killed death."[38] "The Political Life of Dead Bodies" in former socialist countries confirms that the collectively organized memory culture, centred around the names of the dead, has never been livelier in the revisionist mnemonic universe. This especially applies to Slovenia, where, judging by the revisionist efforts to rebury the collaborators' remains, the handling of dead bodies persists as a cultural practice that not only reflects, but also shapes social reality. If true of anyone, it is the Slovenian revisionists who first ventured into the "age of 'necronominalism,'" the age when, according to Thomas Laqueur, "writing and preserving the names of the dead obtain a new significance."[39]

This is one of the main reasons why the term "the haunting past" remains, for the time being, a synonym for the changing national memory. Even more so, after coming under the umbrella of "post-truth historiography," the Slovenian post-socialist revisionist historiography moved beyond its standard premise, according to which historical representation does not necessarily falsify or contest the truth, but rather makes it of secondary importance, therein also beginning to change the historical facts. In some aspects, this might be connected with changes to Slovenian media, whereby I am primarily referring to those changes that enable the fragmentation of sources, and thus create parallel interpretative worlds in which misinterpretation is spread with alarming speed. In a world dominated by an us-versus-them mindset, "our" history is trusted more than any other interpretation. When presented with evidence that contradicts a revisionist narrative, people who choose to believe in it simply ditch the annoying facts.

To avoid oversimplification by stressing the political influence of the revisionist post-truth relativism on post-socialist historiography (and the social sciences), we must be aware that radical reinterpretation and the quest for national reconciliation in countries like Slovenia incorporates several other conflicts. They also involve a struggle over the controlling political analogies. They involve a sharp attack on historians flirting with the social sciences – the latter being related to the realization that memory itself is not a simple act of recall, but a socially constitutive act.

---

37 Susannah Radstone, *Memory and Methodology* (Oxford: Berg Publishers, 2000), 15.
38 Zygmunt Bauman, *Mortality, Immortality, and Other Life Strategies* (Stanford University Press, 1992), 190.
39 Hans Ruin, *The Work of the Dead: A Cultural History of Mortal Remains*. By Thomas Laqueur (Princeton: Princeton University Press, 2015), xix, 711, in *History and Theory. Studies in the Philosophy of History*, Vol. 56, No. 3, September 2017, 407–417.

On the other hand, the advocates of the grass-roots sanitization of the history of the Second World War have also embraced several postmodern criteria regarding what constitutes historical knowledge. For them, what the collaborators did matters far less than how they envisaged the occupation and the war in Europe in general. And the shift that already began in the late 1980s was not just a simple turn to neo-conservatism, but a turn to neo-Historicism and to what Charles Maier would call a "neo-structural functionalism."[40] Nevertheless, the radical reinterpretation or political sanitization of the given past has also enabled a broader public, and the political relativization of responsibility. If fully licensed academics could question whether joining the *Milizia volontaria anticomunista* and the Home Guard was an act of collaboration, or could even claim that these units were actually the representatives of the Slovenian National Army, would not the wider anti-liberal public also be justified in casting off any acceptance of national historical responsibility? Especially if such juggling with the past is supported and even enabled by the country's president.

According to the annual national polls, the majority of Slovenes still reject such a transformation of roles. Although opting for the disintegration of Yugoslavia also rested on critique of the one-sided interpretation of the Second World War and the killing of collaborating Home Guards, Slovenia's independence did not (yet) lead the Slovenes to the relativization of collaborationist evil. What it did do is provoke discussion over the similarities between communism and Nazism.

However, while showing no real interest in relativizing the Nazi crimes, the revisionists only attack those who "collaborated" with communism, or who continue to oppose the interpretation of both totalitarianisms as equal.[41] Similarly to German revisionists forty years previously, their Slovenian epigones, too, believe that the ongoing resistance–collaboration debate polarizes the Slovenes more readily than anywhere else. By doing so and by opting for changes in the status of victimhood, they keep to the memories they find convenient. In their "suffering from a destructive historical fever" (Nietzsche), they have failed to "recognize what they are suffering from," or, even more importantly, are not willing to recognize "reflective memory" as a complex entity. And they are still not prepared or ready to see that "historicization" cannot be used to "confront the past, but to complicate it."[42]

---

40 Charles S. Maier, *The Unmasterable Past. History, Holocaust, and German National Identity* (Cambridge: Harvard University Press, 1988), 171.
41 In the revisionist interpretation, Slovenian communism is presented as monolithic. The authors who condemn it deny the fact that being a communist in Slovenia after the 1960s had next to nothing to do with a desire to establish a regime resembling the one found in the USSR.
42 Ibid., 172.

zeitgeschichte extra

Petra Mayrhofer

Searching for "1989" on the Transnational Remembrance Landscape: A Topography

The year 2019 marks an important anniversary in Europe:[1] it has been thirty years since the system changes in Eastern European communist countries took place in 1989. The following transformation processes were marked by the *dilemma of simultaneity* (*Dilemma der Gleichzeitigkeit*), as political, economic and social systems changed fundamentally and all at the same time.[2] The majority of these countries turned towards integration in Western organisations such as the North Atlantic Treaty Organization (NATO) and the European Union (EU). Furthermore, debates and confrontations with contemporary national history, especially with regard to National Socialist and communist past, started to set in.

Undoubtedly, the 30th anniversary of "1989"[3] will evoke numerous commemoration activities, symbolizing hegemonic remembrance cultures that have already been established. Yet, it is still unknown whether common remembrance patterns will emerge on this occasion. Stepping back to the year 2009, the European Commission produced an official commemoration video entitled "20th Anniversary of Democratic Change in Central and Eastern Europe"; this two-and-a-half minute clip, produced by the Audiovisual Service of the European Commission and published on EU-tube, presented the history of the Enlargement of the EU since 1989, and "effectively assimilated the revolutions of 1989 into the established narrative of west European integration".[4] Accompanying a

---

1 This article bases on Petra Mayrhofer, "Topografie des Erinnerns an '1989'," PhD diss. (University of Vienna, 2017), 194–228. All citations original in another language than English have been translated by the author. I am very thankful to Carmen Gruber for her assistance and valuable comments.
2 Claus Offe, "Das Dilemma der Gleichzeitigkeit. Demokratisierung und Marktwirtschaft in Osteuropa," *Merkur* 505 (1991) 4: 279–92.
3 According to Christoph Boyer, "1989" is used as a "cipher for the event complex" of incidents taking place in 1989 that led to the system changes, see Christoph Boyer, "'1989' und die Wege dorthin," *Vierteljahrshefte für Zeitgeschichte* 59 (2011) 1: 101–18.
4 Stefan Auer, "Contesting the Origins of European Liberty. The EU narrative of Franco-German reconciliation and the eclipse of 1989," in *Osteuropa*, 10 September 2010 <https://www.

storyline about the EU integration process since 1989 is selected footage of historical events of European contemporary history, including the Hungarian Uprising of 1956, the invasion in Prague in August 1968, Wojciech Jaruzelski at the imposition of martial law in Poland in December 1981, the Baltic Chain of August 1989, the fall of the Berlin Wall in November 1989, the Romanian Revolution in December 1989, the withdrawal of Soviet troops from Hungary in 1991 and Lithuania's independence in 1991.

Scientific approaches to the question of remembrance of "1989" have gained little attention until now.[5] For this reason, this article aims to retrace and analyse the transnational similarities of the mnemonic topography concerning these system changes that go beyond national remembrance cultures. The author argues that transnational similarities exist, although different countries have important distinctions in order to be coherent with their national remembrance landscapes of "1989". To gain an understanding of these characteristics, an exemplary study on visual remembrance cultures in Germany, Hungary and the Czech Republic – countries that were affected by the system change and were members of the EU and the NATO in 2009 – has been carried out and selected results will be presented in this article.

I. Remembrance Cultures and "1989"

In cultural studies, there are a variety of scientific approaches to concepts of memory that exist on a collective level.[6] In this paper, the theoretical framework is based on the concept of remembrance culture (*Erinnerungskultur(en)*): according to Christoph Cornelißen, remembrance culture is defined as a "formal generic term for all conceivable forms of conscious memory of historical events, personalities and processes [...] whether of an aesthetic, political or cognitive nature."[7] It encompasses "that area of public communication, symbolic consolidation and practical commemoration of interpretations of historical events

---

zeitschrift-osteuropa.de/hefte/international/eurozine-en/contesting-the-origins-of-european-liberty/> (18 February 2019).
5 Aline Sierp, "1939 versus 1989 – A Missed Opportunity to Create a European Lieu de Mémoire?," *East European Politics and Societies*, 31 (2017) 3: 439–55; 440.
6 See inter alia Ljiljana Radonić and Heidemarie Uhl (eds.), *Gedächtnis im 21. Jahrhundert: Zur Neuverhandlung eines kulturwissenschaftlichen Leitbegriffs* (Bielefeld: transcript, 2016); Aleida Assmann, *Das neue Unbehagen an der Erinnerungskultur: Eine Intervention* (München: Beck, 2013); Astrid Erll, *Kollektives Gedächtnis und Erinnerungskulturen: Eine Einführung*, 3rd ed. (Stuttgart: Metzler, 2017).
7 Christoph Cornelißen, "Erinnerungskulturen," in *Docupedia-Zeitgeschichte*, 22 October 2012 <http://docupedia.de/zg/cornelissen_erinnerungskulturen_v2_de_2012> (18 February 2019).

in which a society deals with events and traditions."[8] For Hans Günther Hockerts, the essential characteristic of remembrance culture is to present the "totality of the non-specific scientific use of history in public – by the most diverse means and for the most diverse purposes."[9] Remembrance cultures are often disseminated through the media, which serves simultaneously as both a medium and an actor in that the act of reporting itself can be defined as an expression of collective memory[10] in order to "create and enable remembrance cultures."[11]

Of interest in this investigation is how remembrance cultures of "1989" are surrounded by hegemonic remembrance cultures on the national as well as on the transnational European level. Karl Schlögel comments that after 1989, post-communist countries have been confronted with a "double experience" in the sense of dealing with their contemporary history;[12] these countries have been primarily confronted with the question of how to deal with the remembrance of National Socialism and the Holocaust firstly, of communism secondly, and of national collaboration with these two regimes thirdly.[13] It is remarkable that after 1989, an "obvious division of European remembrance along the border of the former Iron Curtain" emerged on the European remembrance landscape.[14] While for Western liberal democratic countries, the remembrance of the Holocaust serves as unique point on the remembrance landscape, post-communist countries started the remembrance of the Holocaust in that very sense only after the system changes of 1989. This process of "universalisation"[15] of Holocaust remembrance was also institutionalized in 2002, as the Council of Europe es-

---

8 Habbo Knoch, *Die Tat als Bild: Fotografien des Holocaust in der deutschen Erinnerungskultur* (Hamburg: Hamburger Edition, 2001), 23f.
9 Hans Günther Hockerts, "Zugänge zur Zeitgeschichte: Primärerfahrung, Erinnerungskultur, Geschichtswissenschaft," in *Aus Politik und Zeitgeschichte*, 26 May 2002 <http://www.bpb.de/apuz/26154/zugaenge-zur-zeitgeschichte-primaererfahrung-erinnerungskultur-geschichtswissenschaft?p=all> (18 February 2019), 16.
10 See more detailed Aleida Assmann, "Zur Mediengeschichte des kulturellen Gedächtnisses," in *Medien des kollektiven Gedächtnisses: Konstruktivität – Historizität – Kulturspezifität*, edited by Astrid Erll and Ansgar Nünning (Berlin – New York: de Gruyter, 2004), 45–60.
11 Astrid Erll, *Kollektives Gedächtnis und Erinnerungskulturen: Eine Einführung* (Stuttgart – Weimar: Metzler, 2005), 123–26.
12 Karl Schlögel, "Orte und Schichten der Erinnerung: Annäherungen an das östliche Europa," *Osteuropa* 58 (2008) 6: 13–25, 8.
13 Muriel Blaive et.al. (eds.), *Clashes in European Memory: The Case of Communist Repression and the Holocaust* (Innsbruck – Wien – Bozen: Studienverlag, 2011).
14 Ljiljana Radonić and Heidemarie Uhl, "Zwischen Pathosformel und neuen Erinnerungskonkurrenzen: Das Gedächtnis-Paradigma zu Beginn des 21. Jahrhunderts: Zur Einleitung," in *Gedächtnis im 21. Jahrhundert: Zur Neuverhandlung eines kulturwissenschaftlichen Leitbegriffs*, edited by Ljiljana Radonić and Heidemarie Uhl (Bielefeld: transcript, 2016), 7–28, 15.
15 Daniel Levy and Natan Sznaider, *Erinnerung im globalen Zeitalter: Der Holocaust* (Frankfurt am Main: Suhrkamp, 2001).

tablished as European Day of Remembrance January, 27. Likewise, the United Nations declared this date as International Holocaust Remembrance Day in 2005. As previously mentioned, the transformation countries were simultaneously attempting to come to terms with their recent communist pasts. Debates about the significance of "Gulag memory"[16] in comparison with Holocaust remembrance, including discussions about tendencies to equate the two, were also transferred on the EU level, as in 2004 and 2007 multiple post-communist countries had joined the EU, and climaxed in the EU Parliament's designation of August 23 as "European Day of Remembrance for Victims of Stalinism and Nazism" in 2009.[17] The establishment of this commemoration day expressed these divergent hegemonic approaches concerning the recent past in the East and West. Since then "the relation of these two *competing memories* gains utmost importance within the debates about a European memory."[18]

In this article, hegemonic structures of the national remembrance landscapes that influenced the way "1989" has been remembered are analyzed as follows: above all, it is to be taken into consideration that national remembrance configurations have been determined not only by the way that the National Socialist and communist past has been remembered, but also by the fact that remembrance took place from the ex-post perspective, which was influenced by the development of national transformation processes between 1989 and 2009 as well as by the handling of other national historical events.

The German case is a sort of exception among the transformation countries as the former German Democratic Republic (GDR) joined the former Federal Republic of Germany (FRG). This united Germany is so determined by hegemonic Western remembrance standards with a Holocaust-centered memory regime "that it is difficult for other types of memory regimes to become salient parts of the mnemonic field at all."[19] Therefore, the unification that started with tearing

---

16 Heidemarie Uhl and Sandra Forrester, "Conflicting Cultures of Memory in Europe: New Borders between East and West?," *Israel Journal of Foreign Affairs* 3 (2009) 3: 59–72; Stefan Troebst, "Jalta versus Stalingrad, GULag versus Holocaust: Konfligierende Erinnerungskulturen im größeren Europa," *Berliner Journal für Soziologie* 15 (2005) 3: 381–400, 383.
17 For the evolutionary history of this commemoration day see Uhl and Forrester, "Conflicting Cultures of Memory in Europe," 65–69.
18 Heidemarie Uhl, "Universalisierung versus Relativierung, Holocaust versus GULag: Das gespaltene europäische Gedächtnis zu Beginn des 21. Jahrhunderts," in *Gedächtnis im 21. Jahrhundert: Zur Neuverhandlung eines kulturwissenschaftlichen Leitbegriffs*, edited by Ljiljana Radonić and Heidemarie Uhl (Bielefeld: transcript, 2016), 81–108, 82, accentuation in original.
19 David Art, "Making Room for November 9, 1989? The Fall of the Berlin Wall in German Politics and Memory," in *Twenty Years After Communism. The Politics of Memory and Commemoration*, edited by Michael Bernhard and Jan Kubik (New York: Oxford University Press, 2014), 195–212, 196f.; see also Assmann, "Das neue Unbehagen an der Erinnerungskultur," 67.

down the Berlin Wall on November 9, 1989 cannot be remembered as a founding myth of the united Germany and the meaning of "1989" in the national remembrance landscape underlies the hegemonic remembrance of the Holocaust.

By contrast, Hungary has been characterized by a deep fragmentation of political camps since 1989, with each of them pursuing their own remembrance cultures and memory politics. On the one hand, coming to terms with its National Socialist past in terms of responsibility, collaboration and restitution led to being accepted as a member of the EU in 2004. But on the other hand, rightwing political camps have focused their attention on interpreting the Hungarian nation as a victim of National Socialism and communism.[20] The Holocaust and Hungary's communist past have been equalized, as became obvious upon the establishment of a National Holocaust Day and a day memorializing the victims of communism, both in 2000.[21] Their equal status is also reflected in the way that Hungary's past was presented in the official museum *Terror Háza* in Budapest, which was created in 2002 under the government of Viktor Orbán.[22] In general, the Hungarian Uprising of 1956 and the debates about its meaning determined the path leading up to the system change in 1989; to the present-day, "1956" serves as a central point on the Hungarian remembrance landscape across all ideological divides. In addition, the political right has promoted the idea that the system change is not finished yet, as there has been no profound change among the elites who enabled the transformation from communism to capitalism. In contrast, the political left has avoided the subject altogether and does not respond to this critique. As a result, "1989" has gained little importance on the national remembrance landscape as a topographic reference point in Hungary.

The Czech Republic, on the other hand, have not had a hegemonic debate about the country's National Socialist past after the system change as the Czechs did not collaborate to a great extent,[23] and both the National Socialist occupation and the Holocaust are remembered as a national trauma.[24] Also, the process of coming to terms with its communist past was enabled by a complete overhaul of

---

20 Regina Fritz, *Nach Krieg und Judenmord: Ungarns Geschichtspolitik seit 1944* (Göttingen: Wallstein, 2012), 286.
21 Krisztián Ungváry, "Der Umgang mit der kommunistischen Vergangenheit in der heutigen ungarischen Erinnerungskultur," in *Vergangenheit in der Gegenwart: Vom Umgang mit Diktaturerfahrungen in Ost- und Westeuropa*, edited by Thomas Großbölting and Dirk Hofmann (Göttingen: Wallstein, 2008), 91–100, 91; 97.
22 See inter alia Csilla Kiss, "Divided Memory in Hungary: The House of Terror and the Lack of a Left-wing Narrative," in *Life Writing and Politics of Memory in Eastern Europe*, edited by Simona Mitroiu (Basingstoke: Palgrave Macmillan, 2015), 242–59, 244.
23 Muriel Blaive, "The Czech Republic," in *Authoritarism, History and Democratic Dispositions in Austria, Poland, Hungary and the Czech Republic*, edited by Oliver Rathkolb and Günther Ogris (Innsbruck – Wien – Bozen: Studienverlag, 2010), 91–106, 99.
24 Hildegard Schmoller, "Das Münchner Abkommen als tschechischer Gedächtnisort," PhD diss., (University Vienna, 2010).

the former elites, which was made possible by so-called lustration laws that were enacted – after mass demonstrations in November and December 1989 led to the collapse of communist rule and dissident leader Vaclav Havel became president at the end of that year. Although is ideological variation within Czech political camps, in 2009 there was a consensus about the meaning of "1989" as an important date in Czech recent history.

Despite the national specifics with regards to remembrance of the Holocaust, communism, "1989", and the East-West divide in the remembrance cultures, transnational similarities can be detected, at least in the way that some of these events of "1989" have entered into the visual remembrance landscape.

II. Sources and Methodology

In order to examine the remembrance landscapes of "1989" in Germany, Hungary and the Czech Republic, an analysis of visual representations has been made with the understanding that "the importance of visual culture for remembering can hardly be overestimated," as Astrid Erll postulated.[25] In general, visuals do not only illustrate a historical event but simultaneously provide information that goes beyond the mere content of the image through the inherent composition and narrative structures of visual elements. Horst Bredekamp defines this as "picture act" (*Bildakt*).[26] Regarding the system changes of 1989, Gerhard Paul highlighted the unique importance of visual culture during these revolutions: political changes abandoned communist visual culture and new visual logos and pictures created by the protest movements emerged; this visually signified change.[27] Moreover, print and TV reporting influenced the course of these revolutions in real time.

As Western European mass media reported about the beginning of the system change in Poland and Hungary, this news made its way to GDR, triggering the mass escape of GDR citizens to Hungary, Poland and socialist Czechoslovakia in order to attempt to cross the border to the FRG. People in today's Czech Republic, Slovakia, Bulgaria and Romania could follow the reactions of the USSR to these movements in real-time on TV just before they began their own system changes. This reporting was heavily determined by influential images such as tearing down the Berlin Wall. Globally, the audience as "virtual co-protestors"

---

25 Erll, "Kollektives Gedächtnis und Erinnerungskulturen," 154.
26 Horst Bredekamp, *Theorie des Bildakts*, 3rd ed. (Berlin: Suhrkamp, 2010).
27 Gerhard Paul, *BilderMACHT: Studien zur Visual History des 20. und 21. Jahrhunderts* (Göttingen: Wallstein, 2013), 540.

could prevent, to a certain extent, Soviet interventions.[28] This specific "character of '1989' as a media event" must be taken into special consideration;[29] the visual representations of "1989" have therefore achieved a high degree of recognition in European societies and as such, they can serve as a perfect means for materializing remembrance cultures. Thus, memory journalism – often created on the occasion of anniversaries – can also be described as a form of remembrance culture since it selects those historical dates which have been deemed worthy of remembrance by hegemonic influences in politics and society.[30]

Following this, the sample for the analysis presented here consists of visual representations published in selected quality newspapers and magazines from Germany, Hungary and the Czech Republic in 2009.[31] In that year, newspapers produced various special supplements, series, chronologies and more about the historical events of 1989 as a form of memory journalism. This anniversary coverage was focused on prolific publication of images and visual representations. It featured historical photos as well as photos of commemorative activities of 2009.

A combination of quantitative and qualitative analysis is applied to the image corpus as a methodological framework. In a first step, the image material was structured by means of quantitative image content analysis and quantitative image type analysis; the analysis was amplified in a second step in a mixture of *visual history*, the iconological-iconographic approach, and political iconography. Selected visual representations have been analyzed by categories of "icons" and "iconic image clusters," the latter classified in the sense of "image genres of cultural memory."[32] As in the works of Gerhard Paul, "icons" are standalone visual representations with a high awareness level because of their iconic potential, as they often consist of visual archetypes. Paul also uses the term "media icons" when it comes to icons conveyed by mass media. These are characterized by high emotional potency. There again, "iconic image clusters"

---

28 Gerhard Paul, "Bild und Umbruch: Gedanken aus der Perspektive der 'Visual History'," in *Visualisierungen des Umbruchs: Strategien und Semantiken von Bildern zum Ende der kommunistischen Herrschaft im östlichen Europa*, edited by Ana Karaminova and Martin Jung (Frankfurt am Main: Peter Lang, 2012), 29–45, 41.
29 Philipp Ther, "1989 – eine verhandelte Revolution," in *Docupedia-Zeitgeschichte*, 11 February 2010 <http://docupedia.de/zg/1989?oldid=75501> (18 February 2019).
30 Ilona Ammann, "Gedenktagsjournalismus: Bedeutung und Funktion in der Erinnerungskultur," in *Geschichtsjournalismus: Zwischen Information und Inszenierung*, edited by Klaus Arnold et.al (Berlin [u. a.]: LIT Verlag, 2010), 153–67, 162. (Kommunikationsgeschichte 21).
31 All editions published in 2009 of the following media: Der Spiegel, Frankfurter Allgemeine Zeitung, Süddeutsche Zeitung, Lidové noviny, Právo, Respekt, Magyar Hírlap, Népszabadság, Magyar Narancs.
32 Definitions by Gerhard Paul, "Das Jahrhundert der Bilder: Die visuelle Geschichte und der Bildkanon des kulturellen Gedächtnisses," in *Das Jahrhundert der Bilder: Bildatlas 1949 bis heute*, edited by Gerhard Paul (Göttingen: Vandenhoeck & Ruprecht, 2008), 14–39, 28–32.

consist of several images of similar structure representing a specific theme, but do not include iconic images.[33]

III. Topography of Remembrance of the Transnational Remembrance Landscape

In contrast to the aforementioned EU video, no transnational master narrative of "1989" is present in this sample. The main finding is coherent with the investigation of the historian James Krapfl who analyzed commemoration events about "1989" in 2009 in all Eastern European countries affected by the system changes, concluding that "there was not a consensus about the exact meaning of 1989."[34] However, a certain transnational remembrance can be identified, the characteristics of which depend primarily on the general significance of "1989" within various national remembrance landscapes, broken by the "prism of nations."[35]

3.1 Remembrance Topographic Location 1: Transnational Thematic Coordinates

Indeed, there is a canon of certain historical events that is located on a transnational remembrance landscape of "1989." This is especially true for all those events that involved border crossings and/or triggered system changes in other Eastern European countries, such as cutting through the Iron Curtain at the Austrian-Hungarian border in June 1989, the mass escape of GDR citizens to Hungary in August 1989, tearing down the Berlin Wall in November 1989 and photos of commemoration activities of these historical events in 2009. From the German point of view, these coordinates on the national remembrance landscape are considered as part of their own national history. For Hungary and the Czech Republic, the fact that both countries were indirectly involved in these historical events make them also part of the nation's recent past.

The main coordinate on the transnational landscape is the fall of the Berlin Wall and the commemorations thereof in 2009, primarily the so-called "Festival

---

33 Gerhard Paul, "Europabilder des 20. Jahrhunderts: Bilddiskurse – Bilderkanon – visuelle Erinnerungsorte," in *Bilder von Europa: Innen- und Außenansichten von der Antike bis zur Gegenwart*, edited by Benjamin Drechsel et al. (Bielefeld: transcript, 2010), 255–81, 267.
34 James Krapfl, "Passing the Torch, despite Bananas: The Twentieth-Anniversary Commemorations of 1989 in Central Europe," *Remembrance and Solidarity* (August 2014) 3: 63–102, 64.
35 Paul, "Europabilder des 20. Jahrhunderts," 273.

of Freedom" in Berlin. For this event there was a stage located in front of Brandenburg Gate where TV moderator Thomas Gottschalk interviewed contemporary witnesses to the historical events in 1989. Along the former Berlin Wall from the Reichstag building past the Brandenburg Gate to Potsdamer Platz, 1,000 colorfully painted, larger-than-life polystyrene dominoes were erected. This was a project of the German Goethe Institute, in which children and artists worldwide designed dominoes with drawings themed around past and present political separations. In addition to the hundreds of visitors, a wide range of international politicians took part, including French President Nicolas Sarkozy, Russian President Dimitri Medvedev, British Prime Minister Gordon Brown, US Secretary of State Hillary Clinton, President of the European Commission José Manuel Barroso and President of the European Parliament Jerzy Buzek as representatives of the EU. Protagonists of the system changes were also present; namely the former president of the trade union Solidarność and President of Poland Lech Wałęsa, former Hungarian Prime Minister Miklós Németh and the last head of state of the Soviet Union Michail Gorbačëv. In addition to official speeches and a music programme, the main attraction was the cascade of the dominoes, initiated on both sides, at the eastern end by Lech Wałęsa and Miklós Németh, and at the western end by José Manuel Barroso, Jerzy Buzek and pupils from European schools. The domino effect was the "repetition of the past in event mode."[36] At the end, there were fireworks accompanied by orchestral music that was especially composed for the festival.[37]

In every country in the study sample, newspapers featured at least one photo of the "Festival of Freedom." From a quantitative point of view, these images comprised one fifth of all front pages published in that were on the topic "1989"; for both Germany and the Czech Republic, these types of images were about one quarter of all front pages on the topic "1989".[38] This can be primarily interpreted as a sign that the fall of the Berlin Wall and its effects were remembered as the most sustainable change for the geopolitical situation in Europe since 1989.

---

36 Gerhard Paul, *Das visuelle Zeitalter: Punkt und Pixel* (Göttingen: Wallstein, 2016), 675. (Visual History: Bilder und Bildpraxen in der Geschichte 1).
37 Sebastian Klinge, *1989 und wir: Geschichtspolitik und Erinnerungskultur nach dem Mauerfall* (Bielefeld: transcript, 2015), 377. (Histoire 61).
38 Photo credits: Fabrizio Bensch/Reuters, published in: *Právo*, 10 November 2009, front page; Reuters, published in: *Lidové noviny*, 9 November 2009, front page; Axel Schmidt/AFP, published in: *Lidové noviny*, 9 November 2009, front page; Fabrizio Bensch/Reuters, published in: *Népszabadság*, 9 November 2009, front page and 10 November 2009, front page; Fabrizio Bensch/Reuters, published in: *Magyar Hírlap*, 10 November 2009, front page; Matthias Lüdecke, published in: *Frankfurter Allgemeine Zeitung*, 10 November 2009, front page; dpa, published in: *Süddeutsche Zeitung*, 9 November 2009, front page; Reuters, published in: *Süddeutsche Zeitung*, 10 November 2009, front page.

Thus, the divided city of Berlin was regarded as a symbol of the Cold War in times of East-West confrontation.

From an iconographic point of view, the ceremony was visually presented in a relatively uniform style, with remarkable homogeneity in the images featured; the iconographic image cluster consisted of photos of the domino wall, partly with and partly without Brandenburg Gate in the background of the picture, as well as various motifs of the dominoes standing or fallen.[39] Of the protagonists, only photos of Angela Merkel as host of the commemoration and two former politicians, Lech Wałesa and Michail Gorbačëv were featured. A photo of these three political actors was shown on the front page of newspapers of all three countries:[40] Angela Merkel, Michail Gorbačëv and Lech Wałesa were standing in front of a poster at the site of the commemorations, at the Bösebrücke in Berlin. The picture composition visually unites yesterday with today, not only with the two historical photos taken on November 9, 1989 alongside the 2009 commemoration, but also with the presence of Lech Wałesa and Michail Gorbačëv as historical contemporary witnesses alongside Angela Merkel. Former politicians presented as contemporary witnesses personified the events of that time and "represent a past that has been overcome and rendered harmless."[41] However, as the role of the two politicians in 1989 has been perceived controversially in post-communist Russia and Poland, their staging as contemporary witnesses in this transnational arena symbolizes the power of national remembrance cultures. In the national remembrance cultures of Hungary, Germany and the Czech Republic, these two politicians are remembered as pioneers in tearing down the Berlin Wall and not for the political changes in their home countries.

Besides these predominantly German historical events, a further thematic

---

39 Photo credits: Fabrizio Bensch/Reuters, published in: *Právo*, 10 November 2009, front page; dpa, published in: *Süddeutsche Zeitung*, 31 December 2009, 16; Axel Schmidt/AFP, published in: *Lidové noviny*, 9 November 2009, front page; Jose Giribas, published in: *Der Spiegel*, 47/2009, 19; Matthias Lüdecke, published in: *Frankfurter Allgemeine Zeitung*, 10 November 2009, front page; Fabrizio Bensch/Reuters, published in: *Népszabadság*, 9 November 2009, front page; dpa, published in: *Süddeutsche Zeitung*, 9 November 2009, front page; Jose Giribas, published in: *Süddeutsche Zeitung*, 10 November 2009, 6; N.N., published in: *Magyar Narancs*, Nr. 49–50/2009, 8; MTI/EPA/Wolfgang Kumm, published in: *Magyar Hírlap*, 14 November 2009, 12; Miklós Tenkős, published in: *Népszabadság*, 26 June 2009, 3; Johannes Eisele/Reuters, published in: *Magyar Hírlap*, 31 December 2009, 11.
40 Photo credits: Reuters, published in: *Právo*, 10 November 2009, front page; Fabrizio Bensch/Reuters, published in: *Népszabadság*, 10 November 2009, front page; Fabrizio Bensch/Reuters, published in: *Magyar Hírlap*, 10 November 2009, front page; Reuters, published in: *Süddeutsche Zeitung*, 10 November 2009, front page.
41 Martin Sabrow, "Der Zeitzeuge als Figur der Zeitgeschichte," in *Kommunismusforschung und Erinnerungskulturen in Ostmittel- und Westeuropa*, edited by Volkhard Knigge (Wien – Köln – Weimar: Böhlau, 2013), 117–32, 127. (Europäische Diktaturen und ihre Überwindung. Schriften der Stiftung Ettersberg 19).

coordinate contains the visual remembrance of the system change in Romania, where every sample includes visual references to the Romanian December of 1989, with photos depicting the struggle,[42] Nicolae Ceaușescu, once with his wife,[43] and then his corpse after his execution.[44] The prominent placement of this event on the remembrance landscape is due to the fact that Romania's "1989" was the "antagonistic example of violent upheaval," in contrast to other peaceful system changes.[45] Aside from the violence, the expressive visual language of the Romanian system change and its motifs — tanks versus street fighters, Romanian flags with a hole in the middle where the communist emblem once was, the corpse of Ceausescu, and so on — is a factor. Additionally, "the Revolution on Television" also showed a high degree of visual mediatization as early as 1989 and is therefore well-known.[46] In addition, the Romanian system change occurred at the end of all system changes in 1989. As such, this marks a temporal cornerstone in the transnational remembrance area.

Another main coordinate on the landscape was the commemoration of the GDR citizens who escaped in 1989. The GDR-car Trabant ("Trabi") was in 1989 one of the main means of transportation of GDR refugees willing to leave their country. So, the car was not only an integral part of historical photos published in 2009, but also part of 2009's memorabilia to find in the media sample, such as a stylized bright red Trabi as an element of the special exhibition at the *Terror Háza* in Budapest, as well as photos of Trabis at the celebrations marking the anniversary of the "Pan-European Picnic" and of commemoration Trabi parades in 2009.[47] Hence, on the visual level, the Trabi comes across as a transnational symbol for GDR refugees.

---

42 Photo credits: Profimedia.cz, published in: Respekt, 19–25 October 2009; 62 Profimedia.cz, published in: *Lidové noviny*, 17 December 2009, 12; Daniel Mihailescu/AFP, published in: *Lidové noviny*, 21 December 2009, 11; Reuters/Ullstein Bild, published in: Der Spiegel, 42/2009, 108; Corbis, published in: *Frankfurter Allgemeine Zeitung*, 5 December 2009, 4; Reuters, published in: *Magyar Narancs*, 17 December 2009, 39; Reuters, published in: *Magyar Hírlap*, 24 December 2009, 12; Daniel Mihailescu/AFP, published in: *Népszabadság*, 18 December 2009, front page.
43 Photo credit: Corbis, published in: *Der Spiegel*, 42/2009, 110.
44 Photo credit: AFP, published in: *Lidové noviny*, 29 January 2009, III.
45 Petra Mayrhofer, "United European Memory? Überlegungen zur europäischen Gedächtnislandschaft am Beispiel der Erinnerung an die Systemwechsel 1989," in *Bananen, Cola, Zeitgeschichte: Oliver Rathkolb und das lange 20. Jahrhundert*, edited by Lucile Dreidemy et al. (Wien – Köln – Weimar: Böhlau, 2015), 939–49, 945.
46 Katarzyna Ruchel-Stockmans, "Televised image in/as history: Videograms of a Revolution and the Visibility of the 1989 Changes," in *Visualisierungen des Umbruchs: Strategien und Semantiken von Bildern zum Ende der kommunistischen Herrschaft im östlichen Europa*, edited by Ana Karaminova and Martin Jung (Frankfurt: Peter Lang, 2012), 47–68.
47 Photo credits: Katalin Vencel/MTI, published in: *Magyar Hírlap*, 16 June 2009, 9; Bernadett Szabó, published in: *Népszabadság*, 16 June 2009, 9; László Beliczay/MTI, published in: *Népszabadság*, 27 June 2009, front page; ČTK/AP, published in: *Lidové noviny*, 20 August

All refugee movements via Poland, Hungary and the Czech Republic have been remembered but both quantitatively and qualitatively more extensively in Germany than in Hungary and the Czech Republic, so in the latter cases, only some photos of the refugee movement, mainly those depiction location in their own borders, were represented. In this respect, photos of the GDR refugees in the FRG embassy in Prague have been visually remembered in the Czech Republic. It is remarkable that photos of GDR refugees who climbed over the fences and walls of the embassy were published on the occasion of the twentieth anniversary of "1989" only in the Czech case, but not in Germany or in Hungary. This might be explained by the fact that in Germany the overcoming of walls is iconographically linked to the fall of the Berlin Wall. Motifs of the despair of these refugees are a visual void in the German case, as only pictures of happy refugees are located in the national remembrance area, thereby interpreting unification as a good thing to remember. In Hungary, the GDR refugees are visually represented only during their stay in Hungary, most of all with a photo showing the refugee camp in Budapest-Zugliget. These Czech and Hungarian motifs were missing in the German sample, in which the refugees always come to the FRG in the end, symbolizing on a visual level the unification that followed.

3.2 Remembrance Topographic Location 2: *Iconography of Overcoming*

The transnational remembrance landscape is characterized by a common iconography of the opening and overcoming of borders; in the following, this is referred to as the *iconography of overcoming*, consisting of an "iconography of opening"[48] and an *iconography of breakthrough*. These two components are mainly determined by two iconic motifs: on the one hand, the "iconography of opening" corresponds with the motif of the staged border openings by politicians at the time. On the other hand, the *iconography of breakthrough* is evident in all those motifs of spontaneous, violent border openings by unknown persons and/or crowds of people, for example at the fall of the Berlin Wall or at the

---

2009, 7; Ullstein Bild, published in: Der Spiegel, 45/2009, 54f; Kaiser/Caro/Keystone, published in: *Der Spiegel*, 44/2009, 135; Norbert Michalke/Vario Images, published in: *Der Spiegel*, 11/2009, 154; Andreas Schoelzel/Visum, published in: *Frankfurter Allgemeine Zeitung*, 6 November 2009, 37; Wolfgang Haut, published in: *Frankfurter Allgemeine Zeitung*, 9 November 2009, front page und 24 December 2009, 110; picture alliance/dpa, published in: *Frankfurter Allgemeine Zeitung*, 14 February 2009, 2; Mecom, published in: *Süddeutsche Zeitung*, 27 October 2009, 9; dpa, published in: *Frankfurter Allgemeine Zeitung*, 9 October 2009, 39; Matthias Lüdecke, published in: *Frankfurter Allgemeine Zeitung*, 10 November 2009, 2.

48 Paul, "Europabilder des 20. Jahrhunderts," 272.

breakthrough of the "Gate of Sopron", part of the Iron Curtain between Hungary and Austria.

3.2.1 Iconography of opening

A most striking example of the "iconography of opening" can be seen in the motif of politicians cutting through the Iron Curtain. This political ritual was initiated by cutting through a signal fence on June 27, 1989 at the Austrian-Hungarian border near Klingenbach by the then Foreign Ministers of Austria and Hungary, Alois Mock and Gyula Horn.[49]

This photo can be defined as a "media icon" because of its peculiarities: the political ritual of cutting through a fence was ex-post, staged at a specially created press event. Fifty international TV teams and photographers broadcasted this event via ARD news, even into the homes of GDR citizens.[50] Due to the fact that the dismantling of the Iron Curtain started in May 1989 and the border fortification was nearly removed by the time the cutting was staged, the former Hungarian Prime Minister Miklós Németh later recalled that the fence had even been rebuilt over a length of thirty meters.[51] The actual remaining length of the Iron Curtain is not pictured. In this photograph, since the Iron Curtain is not visually marked by barbed wire, wire mesh or watchtowers, the barrier does not look threatening. Moreover, all of the protagonists are on the same side of the fence "in order to provide the photographers an optimal picture."[52]

But all these fabrications did not at all prevent the motif from gaining an iconic status in the visual remembrance landscape; detached from its actual history of origin, the photo transformed from a symbolic confirmation of a process that was already undertaken,[53] into a visual synonym "for the end of the Iron Cur-

---

49 Photo credits: Bernhard Holzner, published in: *Der Spiegel*, 44/2009, 132; AP/laif, published in: *Süddeutsche Zeitung*, 27/28 June 2009, 7; AP, published in: *Frankfurter Allgemeine Zeitung*, 27 June 2009, 6; N.N., published in: *Magyar Narancs*, 49–50/2009, 8; MTI, published in: *Magyar Hírlap*, 4 May 2009, 4; MTI/EPA/Martin Schutt, published in: *Magyar Hírlap*, 24 August 2009, 10.
50 Herbert Lackner, "Als die große Wende kam," *Profil*, 30 (1999) 27: 36–39, 36.
51 N.N., "Grenzöffnung 1989: 'Es gab keinen Protest aus Moskau'," *Die Presse*, 19 August, 2014, http://diepresse.com/home/zeitgeschichte/3856351/Grenzoeffnung-1989_Es-gab-keinen-Protest-aus-Moskau (18 February 2019).
52 Christoph Kühberger, "1989 im österreichischen Geschichtsunterricht: Über Zeitpunkte und Ikonen," in *Grenzöffnung 1989: Innen- und Außenperspektiven und die Folgen für Österreich*, edited by Andrea Brait and Michael Gehler (Wien – Köln – Weimar: Böhlau, 2014), 469–82, 480. (Schriftenreihe des Forschungsinstitutes für politisch-historische Studien der Dr.-Wilfried-Hauslauer-Bibliothek 49).
53 Helmut Wohnout, "Vom Durchschneiden des Eisernen Vorhangs bis zur Anerkennung Sloweniens und Kroatiens: Österreichs Außenminister Alois Mock und die europäischen Umbrüche 1989–1992," in *Grenzöffnung 1989: Innen- und Außenperspektiven und die Folgen*

tain."⁵⁴ It is evident that the motif "as a narrative abbreviation of a process of change" was restaged for the first time in December 1989: on the initiative of the Czechoslovak Foreign Minister Jiří Dienstbier, the same scene was repeated on the Austrian-Czech border on December 17, 1989 and the German-Czech border on December 23, 1989.⁵⁵ Both events took place after the actual removal of the border fortification, which had started on December 8, 1989.⁵⁶ The political ritual of restaging was even duplicated in 2007 on the occasion of the enlargement of the Schengen Area. Alois Mock, as a personified symbol for the border opening of 1989, again posed for the cameras at the opening of the border bar at the Austro-Hungarian border.⁵⁷

Regarding the transnational remembrance landscape, this photo motif is part of all three countries' samples; the virtual border removal overwrote the actual one on the visual remembrance landscape. Nonetheless, there are some national differences. In Germany, only the original scenario with Alois Mock and Gyula Horn was published. However, this "icon of the end of the West-East division" was remembered as a precondition for the mass escape of GDR citizens in August 1989.⁵⁸ These German politics of remembrance explain why Horn was decorated with the Order of Merit of the Federal Republic of Germany as well as with the Charlemagne Prize, while the photographer Bernhard Holzner, who masterminded the PR event, was awarded the Medal of Merit of the Federal Republic of Germany in April 2009. Yet, the restaging of this political ritual at the Austrian-Czech and at the German-Czech border was not visually remembered in 2009,

---

für Österreich, edited by Andrea Brait and Michael Gehler (Wien – Köln – Weimar: Böhlau, 2014), 185–220, 190. (Schriftenreihe des Forschungsinstitutes für politisch-historische Studien der Dr.-Wilfried-Hauslauer-Bibliothek 49).

54 Petra Mayrhofer, "Symbolisches Durchschneiden des 'Eisernen Vorhangs'. Bildanalysetext zur Abbildung 9 der Ikone 'Eiserner Vorhang', " in *Europäisches Politisches Bildgedächtnis. Ikonen und Ikonographien des 20. Jahrhunderts*, 1 September 2009 <http://www.demokratiezentrum.org/themen/europa/europaeisches-bildgedaechtnis/eiserner-vorhang/abb9-symbolisches-durchschneiden-des-eisernen-vorhangs.html> (19 February 2019).

55 Kühberger, "1989 im österreichischen Geschichtsunterricht," 479.

56 Photo credit: ČTK, published in: *Lidové noviny*, 19 December 2009, 12; ČTK/Archiv, published in: *Lidové noviny*, 30 June 2009, 13; Ivan Blažek, published in: *Právo*, 23 December 2009, 4.

57 Petra Mayrhofer, "'Festung Europa?' Grenzikonographien im europäischen Raum," in *Europabilder: Innen- und Außenansichten von der Antike bis zur Gegenwart*, edited by Benjamin Drechsel et al. (Bielefeld:transcript, 2010), 307–21, 314; N.N., "Symbolische Grenzöffnung im Burgenland," orf.at, 20 December, 2007, http://bglv1.orf.at/stories/244372 (19 February 2019); Petra Mayrhofer, "Erweiterung des Schengen-Raumes: Bildanalyse zur Abbildung 11 der Ikone 'Römische Verträge. Die Europäische Integration als Geschichtserzählung'," in *Europäisches Politisches Bildgedächtnis. Ikonen und Ikonographien des 20. Jahrhunderts*, 1 September 2009 <www.demokratiezentrum.org/themen/europa/europaeisches-bildgedaechtnis/roemische-vertraege/abb11-erweiterung-des-schengen-raumes.html> (19 February 2019).

58 Paul, "BilderMACHT," 384.

"because it was only a kind of second extraction" of the event.[59] In Hungary, the use of this "media icon" was marginalized to little importance in terms of the status of "1989" on the national remembrance landscape. Although the 2009 commemoration ceremony in Budapest with international politicians in attendance was hosted on the same date as 1989's famous PR event, the photo motif with Mock and Horn was not visually remembered to such an extent as in Germany. It is also worth mentioning that protagonist Horn was attributed another role on the national remembrance landscape due to his post-1989 career as Prime Minister whose communist past and activities were a subject of controversy.[60] In the Czech Republic, only the border openings on the Czech border have been remembered,[61] as the national remembrance of "1989" is very narrow and focuses only on the Czech Velvet Revolution and the events in Germany in 1989.

3.2.2 Iconography of Breakthrough

Another integral part of the *iconography of overcoming* is the *iconography of breakthrough*. An example of this iconographic structure is the "iconic image cluster" of photos depicting the mass escape of GDR citizens as they forcibly opened the "Gate of Sopron" at the Austrian-Hungarian border some hours before the "Pan-European Picnic" started on August 19, 1989. These photo motifs differ with regards to the perspectives from which the photos were taken; what is visually remembered is a frontal view of people squeezing through the half-opened gate, as well as a motif in which the gate was opened and some people had already passed through.[62] What all the photos have in common is the visualization of the opening in a violent way by an active, dynamic crowd. All other images that visualize events before and after passing through the "Gate of Sopron" are missing from the transnational remembrance landscape, which includes the Pan-European Picnic itself, and the fact that the Austrian-Hungarian border was closed again for GDR citizens after the Picnic until September 11, 1989.

---

59 Barbara Tóth, "Die Ungarn reichten die Scheren," *Falter*, 51–52/2007, p. 10.
60 N.N., "Systemwandler, Ex-Ministerpräsident von Ungarn, Gyula Horn, verstorben," *Pester Lloyd*, 20 June, 2013, http://www.pesterlloyd.net/html/1325horntot.html (19 February 2019).
61 Photo credit: ČTK, published in: *Lidové noviny*, 19 December 2009, 12; ČTK/Archiv, published in: *Lidové noviny*, 30 June 2009, 13; Ivan Blažek, published in: *Právo*, 23 December 2009, 4.
62 Photo credits: MTI/Reuters, published in: *Magyar Hírlap*, 3 November 2009, front page; MTI, published in: *Magyar Hírlap*, 30 May 2009, 19; MTI, published in: *Magyar Hírlap*, 18. August 2009, 4; Dirk Eisermann/laif, published in: *Süddeutsche Zeitung*, 19 August 2009, 6; Dirk Eisermann/laif, published in: *Frankfurter Allgemeine Zeitung*, 17 August 2009, 3; Dirk Eisermann, published in: *Der Spiegel*, 22/2009, 114f.

Photo motifs of the overcoming of the Berlin Wall are also remembered transnationally: in all three countries, the motif of the so-called "wall woodpecker" can be found.[63] This person, unknown to the public, is photographed from a lateral camera perspective on the west side of the Berlin Wall demolishing it with a tool, knocking out small segments. In the days after November 9, 1989, rows of "wall woodpeckers" lined the Berlin Wall, but the photos that are part of the transnational remembrance landscape are focused on the representation of just one individual versus the wall as a metaphor for the nation overcoming the Soviet communist system. This visual representation of the "wall woodpecker," however, proved to be the only iconoclastic action that was remembered transnationally about "1989." The marginalized visuality of communism can be observed across borders, as "classical icons of upheaval," such as the destruction of earlier communist symbols or the ordered dismantling of communist symbols, monuments or the renaming of streets and so on, are voids on the transnational remembrance landscape.[64] The system changes are visually remembered by means of the *iconography of overcoming*. This is also accompanied by the transnational use of symbolic images, above all in the context of the fall of the Berlin Wall through, for instance, the numerous motifs of people sitting or standing on top of the Berlin Wall.[65]

---

63 Photo credits: LászloNagy/MTI, published in: *Magyar Hírlap*, 12 November 2009, 12; Reproduction from *The Economist* (2), published in: *Právo*, 9 November 2009, front page and 10; Petra Mayrhofer, "Visualisierungen und Narrative des Falls der Berliner Mauer im Ländervergleich," in *Visualisierungen des Umbruchs: Strategien und Semantiken von Bildern zum Ende der kommunistischen Herrschaft im östlichen Europa*, edited by Ana Karaminova and Martin Jung (Frankfurt: Peter Lang, 2012), 69–89, 80f; Karin Liebhart and Petra Mayrhofer, "Visual Narratives of Political Change in European History Textbooks," in *Constructing and Communicating Europe*, edited by Ol'ga Gyárfášová and Karin Liebhart (Berlin [u. a.]: LIT Verlag, 2014), 215–32, 225f.

64 Paul, "Bild und Umbruch," 43; Lucia Halder and Petra Mayrhofer, "Two become One? Visual Memories of Regime Change 1989/1990 in Germany," in *Regime Changes in 20th Century Europe: Reassessed, Anticipated and in the Making*, edited by Marja Vuorinen et al. (Newcastle-upon-Tyne: Cambridge Scholars Publishing, 2016), 263–87, 278; Paul, "BilderMACHT," 555.

65 Photo credits: Stiebing/Süddeutsche Zeitung-Photo, published in: *Süddeutsche Zeitung*, 9 November 2009, 10; dpa, published in: *Süddeutsche Zeitung*, 31 October/1 November 2009, front page; Alexandra Avakian, published in: *Süddeutsche Zeitung*, 31 October/1 November 2009, 8; I. Roerbein, published in: *Der Spiegel*, 03/2009, 26; no Photo credit, published in: *Népszabadság*, 7 May 2009, 9.

IV. Conclusion

The remembrance of the peaceful system changes that took place in Eastern Europe in 1989, appears to be an important coordinate on a transnational remembrance landscape in Germany, Hungary and the Czech Republic, despite many conflicting national hegemonic remembrance cultures after 1945 and despite a form of *competing memories* between Eastern and Western European countries.

Similarities in this transnational remembrance lie in the visual remembrance of transnational events, namely the mass escape of GDR citizens to the West as well as the fall of the Berlin Wall and its commemoration in 2009, which was remembered because of its geopolitically significant effects. Additionally, the violent changes in Romania serve as a counterpoint to the otherwise peaceful changes of 1989. Little attention is paid to the role of relevant political actors, who are primarily presented as contemporary witnesses of the time.

Furthermore, an *iconography of overcoming* can be detected. It is composed of prevalent motifs of politicians cutting through the Iron Curtain as a planned "iconography of opening" on the one hand, and an *iconography of breakthrough*, which includes motifs of violent openings of border gates or unidentified people tearing down the Berlin Wall by unknown person or a crowd of people, on the other. Iconographically, neither classical iconoclastic actions nor visual juxtapositions of photographs from the communist and post-communist epochs are intended to visualize the system changes twenty years later. The system changes are thus marked by a withdrawal of visibility of the former communist system.

Despite the EU commemoration clip, with its explicit narrative of intertwining EU integration with the end of communism in Europe, there is no master narrative on "1989" on the transnational remembrance landscape. Still, much of national remembrance framework of "1989" which focuses mainly on national events is dominated by the way that the remembrance cultures of the Holocaust and of communism are defined. Nonetheless, there is a transnational general agreement "that something meaningful happened in that year," in the sense that "1989 remains a politically potent point of reference in central Europe."[66]

---

66 Krapfl, "Passing the Torch, despite Bananas," 91.

Abstracts

The Memory of Guilt Revisited: The Slovenian Post-Socialist Remembrance Landscape in Transition

Marta Verginella
Political Remake of Slovenian History and Trivialisation of Memory

In her treatise *Truth and politics* (1967), Hannah Arendt analyses the reasons why politics in either totalitarian or democratic systems tend to root in history, and how the attempts of approximation to the political interpretation of the past take place. Based on Arendt's premises and recent findings of István Rév, who studied the political remake of post-communist society, the article analyses the question of divided and conflicting memories or the winners and the defeated of World War II in present day Slovenia. It focuses on the main criteria of the "war of memories", its political actors, chiefly the state and the Church, and it sheds light also on the role of historiography. Long-term historiographic negligence of oral sources and poor familiarity of a great part of Slovenian historians with the historiographic use of autobiographic and oral sources opened the way to trivialisation of testifiers and political use of history in mass media.
Keywords: politics of the past, totalitarianism, oral history, autobiography, war of memories

Bojan Godeša
Slovenian Historiography in the Grip of Reconciliation

The article aims to clarify the interpretational controversies (particularly the period of the 1941–1945 occupation) through the prism of national reconciliation. In Slovenian society, very different evaluations exist of the engagement of

Slovenian political subjects in World War II. This issue has marked Slovenian society for the last thirty years, and its impacts are still felt today. In this context, the author focuses on the presentation of a methodological and ideological model, which is used by a part of the Slovenian historiography trying to rehabilitate the Slovenian political camp – tarnished with collaboration and defeated in 1945 – by promoting the slogan "without the truth, reconciliation is not possible."
Keywords: national reconciliation, myth-against myth principle, rehabilitation

Marko Zajc
The Politics of Memory in Slovenia and the Erection of the Monument to the Victims of All Wars

The article aims to contextualize the erection of the Monument to the Victims of All Wars in Ljubljana (2017) as a complex phenomenon involving the official politics of memory of the Slovenian state, revisionist aspirations, and the ambivalence of the Slovenian public sphere regarding the traumatic past. Why are the concepts of national disunity and national reconciliation so prominent in Slovenian politics? Why was the monument erected and why "no one is pleased with it," as journalists cynically commented after its erection? The memory politics of moderate national reconciliation, supported by the political centre, has its limits: the history of WWII in Slovenia is perceived as a conflict of two more or less equal sides. Achieving equilibrium between the two sides of WWII is not possible because they had a different role in the war, and they are structurally incomparable. This dualism of historical perception prevents the creation of a more plural and complex outlook on the past in the public sphere.
Keywords: politics of memory, traumatic past, national reconciliation, revisionism

Maruša Pušnik
Media-Based Historical Revisionism and the Public's Memories of the Second World War

The article analyses the making of history from the top-down, with a special focus on media representations of World War II, and from the bottom-up, in investigating how people managed the World War II period through their memories. Writing at the intersection of popular memories and media history management, the author examines the position the media occupy in memory battles over Slovenia's contemporary history. The article posits that World War

II, which also once signified a common Yugoslav identity, has become a convenient site for memory battles. The dominant media produce revisionist narratives of World War II, and, in doing so, incite audiences to blur old memories, and form new ones.
Keywords: memory battles, revisionism, media presentation

Oto Luthar
The Sanitation of Slovenian Post-Socialist Memorial Landscape

Furthering the analyses of changes in the post-socialist memorial landscape in Slovenia after 1991, the article aims for the synthesis that includes also the latest shift in this process. In showing that the study of traumatic events connected to WWII poses especially complex problems in representation, the author is pointing out how the process of mourning was (mis-)used as part of post-socialist Slovenian identity politics. Arguing that in supporting the erection of monuments to more than two hundred "victims of communism", the Slovenian revisionist historiography is not only staging the effort to (symbolically and posthumously) restore the dignity of collaborators killed after the war, the author shows in which way those who were collaborating with the Italian and German occupying forces are being systematically transformed in the role of the victims. And how, on the other hand, the real victims, either the partisans or other members of the resistance are depicted as perpetrators. In analysing the revisionist rhetoric the author also shows how the U.S. Embassy in Ljubljana is being dragged in this process as well.
Keywords: revision, memorial landscape, resistance, collaboration, U.S involvement

Petra Mayrhofer
Searching for "1989" on the Transnational Remembrance Landscape: A Topography

Scientific approaches to the question of remembrance of "1989" on a transnational level have gained little attention until now. For this reason, this article aims to retrace the transnational mnemonic topography concerning these system changes. Therefore, an exemplary study on visual remembrance cultures in Germany, Hungary and the Czech Republic has been carried out and selected results will be presented. Methodologically, the research orients itself around an analysis of visual representations published in selected daily and weekly newspapers in 2009, utilizing a mixed-methods approach of both quantitative and qualitative analysis. The author argues that despite the specifics of the national remembrance cultures transnational similarities concerning the remembrance of "1989" can be detected.

Keywords: remembrance cultures, system changes of 1989, visual representations

Rezensionen

Robert Knight, Slavs in Post-Nazi Austria. Carinthian Slovenes and the Politics of Assimilation, 1945–1960, London u. a. 2017, 262 Seiten.

Robert Knight, britischer Historiker und exzellenter Kenner der Geschichte der frühen Zweiten Republik, hat, so scheint es, ein Faible für kontrovers diskutierte Themen der österreichischen Zeitgeschichte. Besonders interessieren ihn die Kontinuitäten zwischen NS-Zeit und der Nachkriegsdemokratie bzw. Österreichs Umgang mit seiner Vergangenheit. Einer größeren österreichischen Öffentlichkeit wurde Robert Knight mit seiner Untersuchung der Haltung der österreichischen Regierung zur Entschädigung der verfolgten und enteigneten Juden bekannt. Die Ergebnisse seiner Studien und die dafür eingesehenen Ministerratsprotokolle aus der Zeit zwischen 1945 und 1952 publizierte er 1988 unter dem Titel „Ich bin dafür, die Sache in die Länge zu ziehen". Seine pointierten Aussagen, auch zur damals noch gängigen Opferthese, führten zu heftiger Kritik und zu Interventionen auf (außen-)politischer Ebene. Seine Arbeiten zur britischen Besatzungspolitik in Österreich wiederum führten Knight bald zu einem weiteren umstrittenen Thema der österreichischen Zeitgeschichte: der Politik gegenüber den Kärntner Slowenen nach 1945.

Bereits Hanns Haas und Karl Stuhlpfarrer mussten in den 1970er-Jahren erfahren, dass die Beschäftigung mit Geschichte der in Kärnten lebenden autochthonen slowenischen Bevölkerung nicht sehr einfach ist. Und damit ist nicht nur die äußerst komplexe Materie oder die Sprachenproblematik gemeint. Anfeindungen gab es für die beiden Historiker und ihre bis heute wegweisende Studie „Österreich und seine Slowenen" (erschienen 1977) von Seiten der Kärntner Landesgeschichtsschreibung, die damals die Deutungshoheit für sich beanspruchte – legendär sind die Konflikte des damaligen Landesarchivdirektors Alfred Ogris mit Karl Stuhlpfarrer –, sowie von Seiten der deutschnationalen Eliten des Landes. Die gegen die beiden Autoren gerichteten Interventionen waren mannigfach. Anerkennung für ihre Arbeit fanden Haas und Stuhlpfarrer schließlich unter der kärntnerslowenischen Bevölkerung und der slowenischen Wissenschaftscommunity. In Österreich jedoch blieb dieser Teil der Geschichte weiterhin ein weißer Fleck. Das Wissen um die hier lebenden autochthonen Minderheiten, aber auch das Wissen um die in den letzten 100 Jahren vor allem gegen die kärntnerslowenische Bevölkerung gerichteten Formen struktureller Gewalt ist bis heute in der Öffentlichkeit gering, auch wenn nach Haas und Stuhlpfarrer immer wieder Historiker und Sozialwissenschaftler wie Andreas Moritsch, Arnold Suppan oder Albert F. Reiterer sich dieser Themen angenommen und publiziert hatten.

Robert Knight untersucht in der vorliegenden Studie ein sehr spezifisches, für die kärntnerslowenische Bevölkerung jedoch folgenschweres Thema, die Kärntner Schul- und Sprachenpolitik von 1945 bis 1960. Im Herbst 1945 wurde auf Landesebene ein vorbildliches Schulmodell entwickelt. Jedes Schulkind innerhalb eines genau definierten Gebietes sollte demnach beide Sprachen verpflichtend erlernen. Auf diese Weise sollten alle Kinder die jeweils andere Kultur kennen und schätzen lernen und in nächster Konsequenz die Gräben, die in den Jahrzehnten zuvor zwischen den beiden Ethnien gezogen wurden, abgearbeitet werden. An über 100 Volksschulen wurde dieses Konzept 1945 eingeführt. Kaum 13 Jahre später bzw. kaum drei Jahre nach Unterzeichnung des Staatsvertrags war dieses Modell wieder Geschichte. Der obligatorische zweisprachige Unterricht wurde abgeschafft. Eltern, die diesen für ihre Kinder weiterhin wünschten, mussten ihre Kinder nun extra anmelden. Vielfach konnten Eltern jedoch dem sozioökonomischen Druck, der auf sie ausgeübt wurde, nicht Stand halten und verzichteten auf die Anmeldung. Was folgte, war ein enormer sprachlicher Aderlass. Denn viele Eltern gaben in der Folge auch das Slowenische als Familiensprache auf. Dies war den Nationalsozialisten, trotz ihrer brutalen Germanisierungspolitik, in dieser Konsequenz nicht gelungen. Anfang des 20. Jahrhunderts hatten noch über 20 Prozent der Kärntner Bevölkerung angegeben, Slowenisch als Alltagssprache zu verwenden, bei der Volkszählung 2001 waren es weniger als drei Prozent.

Trotz dieser engen thematischen und zeitlichen Fragestellung gelingt es Knight einen wenn auch nur in bestimmten Aspekten vertieften Einblick in die Gegebenheiten des Landes zu geben, ermöglicht zugleich aber auch bislang Unverständliches – erinnert sei an die leidige Ortstafeldebatte – verständlicher zu machen. Dies gelingt auch deshalb, weil Knight bei seiner Frage nach dem Warum für das abrupte Ende des Schulmodells sich nicht davor scheut, einen intensiveren Blick in das 19. Jahrhundert und die erste Hälfte des 20. Jahrhunderts zu werfen. Eindrücklich zeigt er, wie das deutschnationale Element im Siedlungsgebiet der kärntnerslowenischen Bevölkerung immer mehr Fuß fasste und dabei von der Unfähigkeit des slowenischen Klerus, auf die Anforderungen der Moderne entsprechend zu reagieren, profitierte. Bis zum sogenannten „Anschluss" 1938 stellte der Klerus einen wichtigen Teil der slowenischen Elite in Politik, Kultur und Genossenschaftswesen.

Im Hauptteil seiner Studie prüft Knight an Hand des Schicksals der zweisprachigen Schulen seine zentralen Thesen und benennt die Beteiligten an diesem Drama. Die Kontinuität der Kärntner Eliten und ihrer Haltung in der sogenannten Minderheitenfrage ist der nur sehr nachlässig durchgeführten Entnazifizierung geschuldet. Hier versagten sowohl die österreichischen Behörden als auch die britische Besatzung vor Ort. Schon bald kooperierte die Militärregierung lieber mit den deutschsprachigen, teilweise auch belasteten Eliten als mit den ehemaligen Kombattanten, die durch die gesellschaftspolitische Umgestaltung Jugoslawiens bald beinahe durchgängig von beiden Seiten als Kommunisten betrachtet wurden. Das lokale Klima unterminierten zudem die offenen Grenzfragen in Kärnten und um Trieste/Trst/Triest sowie die Politik des Kalten Krieges. Die politischen Eliten vor Ort nahmen ihre Verantwortung gegenüber der Minderheit nicht wahr. Im Gegenteil, vor allem lokale ÖVP-Politiker, unter ihnen auch solche, die selbst slowenische Wurzeln hatten, schürten erneut das seit Jahrzehnten vorhandene antislawische Ressentiment und agierten ab 1947 energisch für ein Aus der Zweisprachigkeit im öffentlichen Raum. Unterstützt wurde ihr Bestreben ab 1949 durch den VdU. Der sozialistische Landeshauptmann Wedenig suchte in Wien vergeblich um Unterstützung für das erfolgversprechende Schulkonzept und resignierte nach inszenierten Protesten schließlich im Herbst 1958, indem er den später nach ihm benannten Erlass unterzeichnete und damit das Ende der obligatorischen zweisprachigen Schule einläutete. Die Bundesregierung legalisierte sein Vorgehen im März 1959 mit einem Gesetz.

Robert Knight hat mit „Slavs in Post-Nazi Austria" ein wichtiges und notwendiges Werk vorgelegt, das durch ein sehr umfangreiches Register erschlossen wird. Für ein nichtkärntnerisches Lesepublikum dürfte es vermutlich schwer sein, viele der genannten Personen und auch einige der gebotenen Informationen zu erfassen und zu verorten, zumal sich Knight gelegentlich in seinem umfassenden Detailwissen verliert. Hilfreich wären sicherlich ausführlichere Vorstellungen der Protagonisten und deren Ideen sowie eine straffere Strukturierung des verwendeten Materials gewesen. Gelegentlich sind wichtige erklärende Informationen in dem über 60 Seiten umfassenden Fußnotenapparat versteckt und nicht in den Fließtext eingebaut, wo sie zur leichteren Lesbarkeit hingehörten. Trotz allem ist dem Werk eine große Leserschaft zu wünschen. Zu wünschen wäre die baldige Übersetzung einer durchgesehenen Ausgabe zu einem vernünftigen Preis.

Brigitte Entner

Alfred Pfoser/Andreas Weigl, Die erste Stunde Null. Gründungsjahre der österreichischen Republik 1918–1922, Salzburg/Wien 2017, 359 Seiten.

Den Gründungsjahren der österreichischen Republik würde in der kollektiven Erinnerung unseres Landes durchaus ein stärkerer Stellenwert gebühren. Unterschiedliche historische Narrative über die Zwischenkriegszeit verstellten oft wie ein verhüllender Nebel den Blick auf die Entstehung der Ersten Republik und erschwerten damit eine gemeinsame, sich auf den Gründungsakt der Republik beziehende Erinnerungskultur oder zumindest Ansätze eines Verfassungspatriotismus, wie ihn andere Staaten kennen. Auch in der Sozialdemokratie, die einst den 12. November jährlich mit großen Manifestationen feierte, ist dieser

Tag als Teil ihres Festkalenders inzwischen längst verschwunden. Und es ist eine Ironie der Geschichte, dass ausgerechnet die FPÖ, die aufgrund ihres deutschnationalen Charakters während der 1960er-Jahre gegen die Einführung des österreichischen Nationalfeiertages opponierte, sich heute mit Erfolg als fahnenschwingender Hort eines neuen rot-weiß-roten Patriotismus gerieren und inszenieren kann. Das Buch von Alfred Pfoser und Andreas Weigl schafft hier Abhilfe.

Detailstudien über die behandelten Jahre gibt es en masse – allein das Verzeichnis der von den Autoren rezipierten Literatur umfasst mehrere hundert Titel. Die Stärke der vorliegenden Arbeit zeichnet sich dadurch aus, bei einem hohen Maß an Quellennähe und Anschaulichkeit verschiedenste Aspekte von Politik, Kultur, Ökonomie, Rechtsordnung und sozialen Verhältnissen zu bewerten, zu problematisieren und für weitergehende Diskussion aufzubereiten. Nicht zuletzt bietet das eine fundierte Grundlage, Wurzeln und Genesis nachfolgender Katastrophen österreichischer Geschichte gründlicher erfassen und verstehen zu können.

Die beiden Autoren haben Widersprüche deutlich herausgearbeitet. In einem Land der gescheiterten Aufstände und Revolutionen brachten die Jahre von 1918 bis 1920 für Österreich so etwas wie einen einzigartigen Quantensprung des gesellschaftlichen Fortschritts, den es in diesen Dimensionen nie zuvor und nie danach gegeben hat: Der Übergang von der Monarchie zur Republik, die Etablierung eines parlamentarischen Regierungssystems, das Frauenwahlrecht, gewaltige sozialpolitische Errungenschaften (Kranken- und Arbeitslosenversicherung, Arbeiterurlaub, Achtstundentag, Betriebsrätegesetz, Schaffung von Arbeiterkammern) und eine demokratische Verfassung, die bis heute Bestand hat. Auf der anderen Seite war es eine Zeit größter Not und beginnender politischer und kultureller Gegensätze, die eine gemeinsame Aufbruchstimmung verhinderten. Und die durch die Umbrüche ausgelöste Reformdynamik kam nach dem Zerfall der Koalition zwischen Christlichsozialen und Sozialdemokraten 1920 zum Erliegen und konnte in der Folge nur noch im „Roten Wien" mit beachtlichen Resultaten fortgeführt werden.

Pfoser und Weigl haben die thematischen Blöcke ihres Buches „Aufbrüche – Niederlagen – Kulturkämpfe" benannt, hinter denen sie die jeweiligen Abhandlungen gruppieren. Die Autoren unternehmen dabei eine anregende und instruktive Tour d'Horizon durch die Problemfelder der ersten Nachkriegszeit.

Zusammenbruch und Zerfall der Österreichisch-Ungarischen Monarchie schufen nicht nur ein zentraleuropäisches Machtvakuum, sondern führten auch zur Auflösung des gemeinsamen Wirtschaftsraumes. Der „Anschluss" an Deutschland schien zum Allheilmittel für die Lösung offener Fragen zu werden. Auch das Anschlussverbot des Friedensvertrages von Saint Germain tat dem keinen Abbruch – die Anschlussaktivitäten verlagerten sich bloß von bundesstaatlicher Ebene auf jene der Länder, wie diesbezügliche Abstimmungen in Tirol und Salzburg demonstrierten.

Seuchen (Spanische Grippe, Tuberkulose), Ernährungslage und Versorgungsdefizite brachten das Land an den Rand einer humanitären Katastrophe. Internationale Hilfslieferungen konnten noch das Schlimmste verhindern. Die hungernden Städte mussten ernährt werden. Damit war auch die Basis für den nachhaltigen Gegensatz zwischen Stadt und Land geschaffen, der in der Folge durch politische und kulturelle Differenzen noch vertieft wurde. Es verschärften sich Ressentiments und oftmals blanker Hass gegen den „Wasserkopf" Wien.

Durch ein neues Frauenbild, die moderne urbane Kultur, Sport, Theater und Kino fühlten sich all jene herausgefordert, die dahinter Sittenverfall und einen Angriff auf die traditionellen Stützen der Gesellschaft witterten. Die katholische Kirche verfügte noch immer – besonders in ländlichen Regionen – über enorme Mobilisierungskraft und konnte sich etwa bei der Verhinderung der obligatorischen Zivilehe, die Scheidungen ermöglicht hätte, erfolgreich behaupten. Der politische Katholizismus spaltete die Gesellschaft und trug nicht zuletzt mit der Intensivierung des Kulturkampfes seinen Teil an Verantwortung für die Destabilisierung der Ersten Republik.

Das Kapitel „Der Jud ist schuld!" gibt einen beklemmenden Einblick in die verstärkte Ausbreitung eines sich radikalisierenden Antisemitismus, der von Christlichsozialen, Großdeutschen und Nationalsozialisten mit unterschiedlichen Nuancen ständig instrumentalisiert wurde. Eine maßlose Hetzkampagne gegen ostjüdische Flüchtlinge erschwerte jenen die Option für Österreich und die Erlangung der Staatsbürgerschaft, was teilweise zu Ausweisungen führte. Antisemitismus beeinflusste ebenso den Kulturkampf: 1921 wollte die christlichsozial-großdeutsche Regierungskoalition die Aufführung von Schnitzlers „Reigen" verbieten, scheiterte aber am Widerstand des Wiener Bürgermeisters Reumann. Und der Schriftsteller Hugo Bettauer war eines der ersten Mordopfer antisemitischer Stimmungsmache.

Die Sozialdemokratie wurde als „Judenschutztruppe" attackiert und verteidigte sich mitunter zwiespältig: Zwar wurde der Antisemitismus entschieden verurteilt, aber auch die Kooperation der christlichsozial geführten Regierung mit „jüdischem Kapital" kritisiert und deshalb die Christlichsozialen des „Schwindelantisemitismus" bezichtigt. Mit solcher Argumentation wurden zugleich die Ressentiments jener bestätigt, die Judentum und Kapital gleichsetzten. Jüdinnen und Juden wurden aus Turn- und Alpinvereinen ausgeschlossen und konnten sich angesichts regelmäßiger Prügelexzesse an den Universitäten und Hochschulen nicht mehr sicher fühlen.

Eine galoppierende Inflation beraubte vor allem den Mittelstand aller Sicherheitsgefühle. Dazu gesellte sich eine Angst vor Umsturz und Kommunismus. Derlei Phobien sollten wenig später als politischen Ausweg die Beseitigung des vermeintlich „revolutionären Schutts" ersehnen und diesen ein Jahrzehnt danach auch exekutieren. Die stabilisierende, letztlich staatstragende Rolle der Sozialdemokratie in der „Ersten Stunde Null" blieb nicht nur unbedankt – im Zuge jener „Aufräumarbeiten" wurde neben der parlamentarischen Demokratie auch die Sozialdemokratie als einzige politische Kraft, die uneingeschränkt die Republik bejahte, mit Gewalt beseitigt.

Ansprechend ist auch der Exkurs „Drei Schriftsteller und die ‚Österreichische Idee'". Hofmannsthal, gegenüber der Republik reserviert bleibend und strikter Gegner eines „Anschlusses" an das Deutsche Reich, versuchte seine während der letzten Jahre der Monarchie kultivierte „Österreichische Idee" als „nationalen Kosmopolitismus" bei den Salzburger Festspielen weiterzuführen.

Für Robert Musil waren nationale Ideen nichts anderes als ideologische „Blendgranaten". Deutschtümelei und Österreichertum waren ihm daher gleichermaßen fremd, wenngleich er aus pragmatischen Gründen eine Vereinigung mit Deutschland bevorzugt hätte.

Unter den Schriftstellern gab es keinen engagierteren Republikaner als Karl Kraus. Allein schon die Verabscheuung im Monumentaldrama „Die letzten Tage der Menschheit" so eindringlich dokumentierten Grausamkeiten war Triebkraft für sein rastloses Wirken, das ihn während jener Jahre an die Seite der Sozialdemokratie führte, an deren Republikfeiern er stets mitwirkte. Bei aller sonstigen wissenschaftlichen Distanz der Autoren bricht bei der Würdigung von Kraus große Sympathie durch: „In seiner analytischen Unbeugsamkeit war er von allen österreichischen Schriftstellern der Begnadetste, Österreich mit aller Kraft zu schmähen und gleichzeitig mit unbändiger Liebe zu ihm verbunden zu sein" (248).

„Die erste Stunde Null" ist ein gelungener, angemessener und wichtiger Beitrag zum 100-jährigen Jubiläum der Republik Österreich.

Heimo Gruber

Günter Bischof/Hans Petschar, Der Marshallplan. Die Rettung Europas und der Wiederaufbau Österreichs. Das europäische Wiederaufbauprogramm, der ERP-Fonds, die Marshallplan-Jubiläumsstiftung, Wien 2017, 333 Seiten, mit Abbildungen.

„Wer schnell hilft, hilft doppelt." Mit diesem Sprichwort könnte die Wirkung des Marshallplanes für Österreich recht treffend umschrieben werden. Was der kriegsgeschädigten österreichischen Wirtschaft fehlte, um nach 1945 wieder in Gang zu kommen, waren vor allem Rohstoffe und Maschinen, die aus Mangel an Devisen nur unzureichend aus dem Ausland bezogen werden konnten. Nachdem dann mit Hilfe des Marshallplanes diese Engpässe überwunden waren, gelang es der österreichischen Wirtschaft ab den 1950er-Jahren, in zunehmendem Maße ohne fremde Hilfe auf die heimische wie internationaler Nachfrage nach Gütern aller Art zu reagieren. Der damit verbundene Aufschwung der österreichischen Wirtschaft wäre jedoch ohne die frühe Unterstützung aus dem Marshallplan zweifellos schwieriger und langsamer erfolgt – und möglicherweise mit stärkeren sozialen Verwerfungen einhergegangen.

Die Marshallplan-Hilfe, die am 5. Juni 1947 vom amerikanischen Außenminister George C. Marshall in einer Rede an der Harvard University angekündigt und in den folgenden Jahren im nicht-kommunistischen Europa umgesetzt wurde, bestand in Österreich – neben der Werbung für Demokratie und den American way of life – vor allem aus zwei Elementen: zum einen in der kostenlosen Bereitstellung der erforderlichen Güter aus den USA, die dann von der österreichischen Regierung gegen inländische Zahlungsmittel an die einzelnen Unternehmen verkauft wurden; und zum anderen in der Anhäufung der daraus erzielten Erlöse im sogenannten ERP-Fonds (European Recovery Program), aus dem in der weiteren Folge und bis heute kostengünstige Kredite im Ausmaß von umgerechnet über 15 Milliarden Euro an die österreichische Wirtschaft vergeben wurden. Österreich erhielt dabei gemessen an der Bevölkerungsgröße einen überproportional hohen Anteil an der gesamten von den USA an Europa geleisteten Hilfe, was mit der aus der Anwesenheit sowjetischer Besatzungstruppen resultierenden Sonderstellung begründet wurde. Und tatsächlich entsprach der Wert der für Österreich bestimmten Hilfe in etwa dem Schaden, der aus den Demontagen und den von den Sowjets erzwungenen Lieferungen in die Sowjetunion entstand.

All dies und vieles mehr wird von Günter Bischof und Hans Petschar in Wort und Bild in einem großformatigen Jubiläumsband festgehalten, der anlässlich von 70 Jahren Marshallplan herausgegeben wurde und in seiner überaus aufwändigen Gestaltung durchaus dessen einzigartigen Bedeutung entspricht. Dabei dienen die zahlreichen Abbildungen, die von Hans Petschar zusammengestellt wurden, nicht nur der Illustration des von Günter Bischof verfassten Textes, sondern erzählen ihrerseits und gewissermaßen autonom die Geschichte des Marshallplanes in Österreich und zum Teil auch in Europa. Dank umfangreicher Recherchen bietet der Band für die Wissenschaft ebenso wie für die breite Öffentlichkeit eine gelungene Aufarbeitung des Marshallplanes und seiner Auswirkungen. Dank seiner gefälligen Gestaltung mit hunderten von Bildern, Karten und Grafiken eignet er sich als passendes Geschenk für welchen Anlass auch immer. Sie reflektieren die Geschehnisse auf dem politischen Parkett ebenso wie die Aktivitäten in der wiederaufgebauten Wirtschaft oder die unmittelbaren Erlebnisse und Erfahrungen der Bevölkerung mit dem Marshallplan. In den neben Einleitung und Anhang insgesamt 20 Kapiteln werden verschiedene Facetten des Marshallplanes detailreich beleuchtet, wobei der Großteil der Ausführungen naturgemäß auf die Jahre 1948 bis 1952 entfällt. In diese Zeit fallen die entscheidenden Verhandlungen und Hilfslieferungen, die sich dank des amerikanischen Kontrollbedürfnisses zwar nicht problemlos gestalteten, im Falle Österreichs jedoch durch bereits zuvor ausgearbeitete Investitionspläne ganz wesentlich erleichtert wurden. Ihre Darstellung ist stets auch eingebettet in die sowohl außen- als auch innenpolitischen Rahmenbedingungen, die bei der Umsetzung der Hilfe zu berücksichtigen waren. Dabei gab es auf beiden Seiten, in den USA ebenso wie in Europa, durchaus auch Widerstände zu überwinden. Zuletzt kommt auch das Weiterleben des Marshallplanes bis in die Gegenwart zur Sprache, und zwar in den Mitteln des ERP-Fonds ebenso wie in der Erinnerungskultur und zuletzt auch in der Gründung einer Marshallplan-Jubiläumsstiftung im Jahre 1999, die sich der weiteren Pflege der transatlantischen Beziehungen widmet.

Gerade in Zeiten, in denen das Verhältnis Europas zu den USA eine gewisse Abkühlung erfahren hat, tut es gut, an die Jahre der für beide Seiten fruchtbaren Kooperation erinnert zu werden. Auch wenn diese keinesfalls konfliktfrei verlief, waren die USA trotz aller Eigeninteressen wie etwa der Öffnung des europäischen Marktes für die amerikanische Wirtschaft in einem hohen Maße um eine Integration der europäischen Länder bemüht – ein Engagement, das man sich heutzutage nicht nur für Europa wünschen würde.

Franz Mathis

Autor/inn/en

Brigitte Entner, Mag.
Klagenfurt

Bojan Godeša, Dr.
Senior researcher at the Institute of Contemporary History, Ljubljana, bojan.godesa@inz.si

Heimo Gruber
Wien

Oto Luthar, Dr.
Senior researcher at the Research Centre of the Slovenian Academy of Sciences and Arts (ZRC SAZU), Institute of Culture and Memory Studies in Ljubljana, luthar@zrc-sazu.si

Franz Mathis, Univ.-Prof. Dr.
Institut für Geschichtswissenschaften und Europäische Ethnologie, Universität Innsbruck, franz.mathis@uibk.ac.at

Petra Mayrhofer, Dr.
Institut für Zeitgeschichte der Universität Wien, petra.mayrhofer@univie.ac.at

Maruša Pušnik, Dr.
Associate professor at the University of Ljubljana, Faculty of Social Sciences, marusa.pusnik@fdv.uni-lj.si

Heidemarie Uhl, Priv. Doz. Mag. Dr. phil.
Senior researcher at the Austrian Academy of Sciences, Institute for Culture Studies and History of Theater/Cluster "Sites of Memory", heidemarie.uhl@oeaw.ac.at

Marta Verginella, Prof.
Professor at the Faculty of Arts, University of Ljubljana, Department of History,
verginella@ff.uni-lj.si

Marko Zajc, Dr.
Associate researcher at the Institute of Contemporary History, Ljubljana,
marko.zajc@inz.si

Zitierregeln

Bei der Einreichung von Manuskripten, über deren Veröffentlichung im Laufe eines doppelt anonymisierten Peer Review Verfahrens entschieden wird, sind unbedingt die Zitierregeln einzuhalten. Unverbindliche Zusendungen von Manuskripten als word-Datei an: agnes.meisinger@univie.ac.at

I. Allgemeines

Abgabe: elektronisch in Microsoft Word DOC oder DOCX.

Textlänge: 60.000 Zeichen (inklusive Leerzeichen und Fußnoten), Times New Roman, 12 pt, 1 $\frac{1}{2}$-zeilig. Zeichenzahl für Rezensionen 6.000–8.200 Zeichen (inklusive Leerzeichen).

Rechtschreibung: Grundsätzlich gilt die Verwendung der neuen Rechtschreibung mit Ausnahme von Zitaten.

II. Format und Gliederung

Kapitelüberschriften und – falls gewünscht – Unterkapiteltitel deutlich hervorheben mittels Nummerierung. Kapitel mit römischen Ziffern [I. Literatur], Unterkapitel mit arabischen Ziffern [1.1 Dissertationen] nummerieren, maximal bis in die dritte Ebene untergliedern [1.1.1 Philologische Dissertationen]. Keine Interpunktion am Ende der Gliederungstitel.

Keine Silbentrennung, linksbündig, Flattersatz, keine Leerzeilen zwischen Absätzen, keine Einrückungen; direkte Zitate, die länger als vier Zeilen sind, in einem eigenen Absatz (ohne Einrückung, mit Gänsefüßchen am Beginn und Ende).

Zahlen von null bis zwölf ausschreiben, ab 13 in Ziffern. Tausender mit Interpunktion: 1.000. Wenn runde Zahlen wie zwanzig, hundert oder dreitausend nicht in unmittelbarer Nähe zu anderen Zahlenangaben in einer Textpassage aufscheinen, können diese ausgeschrieben werden.

Daten ausschreiben: „1930er" oder „1960er-Jahre" statt „30er" oder „60er Jahre".

Datumsangaben: In den Fußnoten: 4. 3. 2011 [Leerzeichen nach dem Punkt, nicht 04.03. 2011 oder 4. März 2011]; im Text den Monat ausschreiben [4. März 2011].

Personennamen im Fließtext bei der Erstnennung immer mit Vor- und Nachnamen.

Namen von Organisationen im Fließtext: Wenn eindeutig erkennbar ist, dass eine Organisation, Vereinigung o. Ä. vorliegt, können die Anführungszeichen weggelassen werden: „Die Gründung des Oesterreichischen Alpenvereins erfolgte 1862." „Als Mitglied im Womens Alpine Club war ihr die Teilnahme gestattet." **Namen von Zeitungen/Zeitschriften** etc. siehe unter „Anführungszeichen".

Anführungszeichen im Fall von Zitaten, Hervorhebungen und bei Erwähnung von Zeitungen/Zeitschriften, Werken und Veranstaltungstiteln im Fließtext immer doppelt: „"

Einfache Anführungszeichen nur im Fall eines Zitats im Zitat: „Er sagte zu mir: ‚….'"

Klammern: Gebrauchen Sie bitte generell runde Klammern, außer in Zitaten für Auslassungen: […] und Anmerkungen: [Anm. d. A.].

Formulieren Sie **bitte geschlechtsneutral bzw. geschlechtergerecht.** Verwenden Sie im ersteren Fall bei Substantiven das Binnen-I („ZeitzeugInnen"), nicht jedoch in Komposita („Bürgerversammlung" statt „BürgerInnenversammlung").

Darstellungen und Fotos als eigene Datei im jpg-Format (mind. 300 dpi) einsenden. Bilder werden schwarz-weiß abgedruckt; die Rechte an den abgedruckten Bildern sind vom Autor/von der Autorin einzuholen. Bildunterschriften bitte kenntlich machen: Bild: Spanische Reiter auf der Ringstraße (Quelle: Bildarchiv, ÖNB).

Abkürzungen: Bitte Leerzeichen einfügen: vor % oder €/zum Beispiel z. B./unter anderem u. a. Im Text sind möglichst wenige allgemeine Abkürzungen zu verwenden.

III. Zitation

Generell keine Zitation im Fließtext, auch keine Kurzverweise. Fußnoten immer mit einem Punkt abschließen.

Die nachfolgenden Hinweise beziehen sich auf das Erstzitat von Publikationen. Bei weiteren Erwähnungen Kurzzitat. Wird hintereinander aus demselben Werk zitiert bitte den Verweis „Ebd." bzw. mit anderer Seitenangabe „Ebd., 12." gebrauchen. Kein „Ders./ Dies." Zwei Belege in einer Fußnote mit „;" trennen: Gehmacher, Jugend, 311; Dreidemy, Kanzlerschaft, 29. Bei Übernahme von direkten Zitaten aus der Fachliteratur „Zit. n." verwenden.

Monografien: Vorname und Nachname, Titel, Ort und Jahr, Seitenangabe [ohne „S."].
Beispiel Erstzitat: Johanna Gehmacher, Jugend ohne Zukunft. Hitler-Jugend und Bund Deutscher Mädel in Österreich vor 1938, Wien 1994, 311.
Beispiel Kurzzitat: Gehmacher, Jugend, 311.
Bei mehreren AutorInnen/HerausgeberInnen: Dachs/Gerlich/Müller (Hg.), Politiker, 14.

Reihentitel: Claudia Hoerschelmann, Exilland Schweiz. Lebensbedingungen und Schicksale österreichischer Flüchtlinge 1938 bis 1945 (Veröffentlichungen des Ludwig-Boltzmann-Institutes für Geschichte und Gesellschaft 27), Innsbruck/Wien [bei mehreren Ortsangaben Schrägstrich ohne Leerzeichen] 1997, 45.

Dissertation: Thomas Angerer, Frankreich und die Österreichfrage. Historische Grundlagen und Leitlinien 1945–1955, phil. Diss., Universität Wien 1996, 18–21 [keine ff. und f. für Seitenangaben, von–bis mit Gedankenstrich ohne Leerzeichen].

Diplomarbeit: Lucile Dreidemy, Die Kanzlerschaft Engelbert Dollfuß' 1932–1934, Dipl. Arb., Université de Strasbourg 2007, 29.

Ohne AutorIn, nur HerausgeberIn: Beiträge zur Geschichte und Vorgeschichte der Julirevolte, hg. im Selbstverlag des Bundeskommissariates für Heimatdienst, Wien 1934, 13.

Unveröffentlichtes Manuskript: Günter Bischof, Lost Momentum. The Militarization of the Cold War and the Demise of Austrian Treaty Negotiations, 1950–1952 (unveröffentlichtes Manuskript), 54–55. Kopie im Besitz des Verfassers.

Quellenbände: Foreign Relations of the United States, 1941, vol. II, hg. v. United States Department of States, Washington 1958.
[nach Erstzitation mit der gängigen Abkürzung: FRUS fortfahren].

Sammelwerke: Herbert Dachs/Peter Gerlich/Wolfgang C. Müller (Hg.), Die Politiker. Karrieren und Wirken bedeutender Repräsentanten der Zweiten Republik, Wien 1995.

Beitrag in Sammelwerken: Michael Gehler, Die österreichische Außenpolitik unter der Alleinregierung Josef Klaus 1966–1970, in: Robert Kriechbaumer/Franz Schausberger/Hubert Weinberger (Hg.), Die Transformation der österreichischen Gesellschaft und die Alleinregierung Klaus (Veröffentlichung der Dr.-Wilfried Haslauer-Bibliothek, Forschungsinstitut für politisch-historische Studien 1), Salzburg 1995, 251–271, 255–257.
[bei Beiträgen grundsätzlich immer die Gesamtseitenangabe zuerst, dann die spezifisch zitierten Seiten].

Beiträge in Zeitschriften: Florian Weiß, Die schwierige Balance. Österreich und die Anfänge der westeuropäischen Integration 1947–1957, in: Vierteljahrshefte für Zeitgeschichte 42 (1994) 1, 71–94.
[Zeitschrift Jahrgang/Bandangabe ohne Beistrichtrennung und die Angabe der Heftnummer oder der Folge hinter die Klammer ohne Komma].

Presseartikel: Titel des Artikels, Zeitung, Datum, Seite.
Der Ständestaat in Diskussion, Wiener Zeitung, 5. 9. 1946, 2.

Archivalien: Bericht der Österr. Delegation bei der Hohen Behörde der EGKS, Zl. 2/pol/57, Fritz Kolb an Leopold Figl, 19. 2. 1957. Österreichisches Staatsarchiv (ÖStA), Archiv der Republik (AdR), Bundeskanzleramt (BKA)/AA, II-pol, International 2 c, Zl. 217.301-pol/57 (GZl. 215.155-pol/57); Major General Coleman an Kirkpatrick, 27. 6. 1953. The National Archives (TNA), Public Record Office (PRO), Foreign Office (FO) 371/103845, CS 1016/205 [prinzipiell zuerst das Dokument mit möglichst genauer Bezeichnung, dann das Archiv, mit Unterarchiven, -verzeichnissen und Beständen; bei weiterer Nennung der Archive bzw. Unterarchive können die Abkürzungen verwendet werden].

Internetquellen: Autor so vorhanden, Titel des Beitrags, Institution, URL: (abgerufen Datum). Bitte mit rechter Maustaste den Hyperlink entfernen, so dass der Link nicht mehr blau unterstrichen ist.
Yehuda Bauer, How vast was the crime, Yad Vashem, URL: http://www1.yadvashem.org/yv/en/holocaust/about/index.asp (abgerufen 28. 2. 2011).

Film: Vorname und Nachname des Regisseurs, Vollständiger Titel, Format [z. B. 8 mm, VHS, DVD], Spieldauer [Film ohne Extras in Minuten], Produktionsort/-land Jahr, Zeit [Minutenangabe der zitierten Passage].
Luis Buñuel, Belle de jour, DVD, 96 min., Barcelona 2001, 26:00–26:10 min.

Interview: InterviewpartnerIn, IntervieweIn, Datum des Interviews, Provenienz der Aufzeichnung.
Interview mit Paul Broda, geführt von Maria Wirth, 26.10.2014, Aufnahme bei der Autorin.

Die englischsprachigen Zitierregeln sind online verfügbar unter: https://www.verein-zeitgeschichte.univie.ac.at/fileadmin/user_upload/p_verein_zeitgeschichte/zg_Zitierregeln_engl_2018.pdf

Es können nur jene eingesandten Aufsätze Berücksichtigung finden, die sich an die Zitierregeln halten!